Francois Tott

Memories of the Baron de Tott, on the Turks and the Tartars

Francois Tott

Memories of the Baron de Tott, on the Turks and the Tartars

ISBN/EAN: 9783743395268

Manufactured in Europe, USA, Canada, Australia, Japa

Cover: Foto ©ninafisch / pixelio.de

Manufactured and distributed by brebook publishing software (www.brebook.com)

Francois Tott

Memories of the Baron de Tott, on the Turks and the Tartars

M E M O I R S

O F T H E

BARON DE TOTT.

SECOND PART.

On the TURKS, *and the* TARTARS.

MY Father died at Rodofto †, in the arms of Count Tezaky, and in the midft of his countrymen. The Miniftry which had intended to have

† A town fituated on the Propontis; fet apart by the Grand S gnior for the refidence of Prince Ragotzi, and all the Hungarian refugees. My deceafed father had followed that Prince thither, and left it in the year 1717, to enter into the fervice of France: the different commiffions in which he was employed, gave him frequent opportunities of feeing his former companions, in the midft of whom he died in 1757. Count Tezaky furvived him only eight days, and never fpoke after his death.

VOL. II.   B   employed

employed me, had juft been changed in
France. A foreign name, no protection,
and eight years abfence at Conftantinople,
nothing, in fhort, feemed to give me much
profpect of fuccefs at Verfailles. I obtained,
however, a promife of employment at one
of the German Courts, an employment ill-
fuited to the fort of information I had ac-
quired, and which the Duke of Choifeul
was defirous of applying to more purpofe,
when on his refuming the foreign depart-
ment, and after a trial of my abilities on a
particular commiffion, he made choice of
me to refide with the Kam of the Tartars.
My zeal made me overlook all the difagreeable circumftances of fuch a miffion. I
had neither folicited, nor defired, nor forefeen it; but I accepted it as a favour, and
it was indeed a favour to ferve under that
Minifter.

It was determined that I fhould go by
land to the place of my deftination, and
every thing being prepared, I left Paris on
the 10th of July, 1767, for Vienna, where,
after a ftay of eight days, I continued my
journey to Warfaw, at which place I remained

mained fix weeks, and from thence I proceeded to Kaminiek.

The difficulties I had undergone in Poland from the fcarcity of provifions, the
want of horfes, and the ill will of the people, prepared me to bear, with patience,
what I ftill had to undergo before I could
arrive at the end of my journey.

There being no poft-horfes in Poland,
after paffing Kaminiek, I was fortunate
enough to procure Ruffian horfes to carry
me to the firft Turkifh Cuftom-houfe, oppofite to Swanitz, on the other fide of the
Niefter. The courfe of that river forms
the boundary between the two empires;
and fome Janiffaries who were come to
walk on the Polifh fide of the river, at-
tracted by curiofity near my carriage, taking a liking to me on my addreffing them
in the Turkifh language, accompanied me
in the ferry boat, which conveyed us to
the other fide. Every perfon in my retinue, except my fecretary, imagined we
were going to Conftantinople. I undeceived them in paffing the Niefter ‡. We

‡ This river is alfo called the Nieper.

B 2   landed

landed· fafely on the oppofite fide of the
river, and my Janiffaries, eager to acquaint the Cuftom-houfe Officer with my
arrival, prepared him to receive me with
fo much refpect, that, overcome at length
by his entreaties, I agreed to pafs a bad
night at about a league from Kotchim,
where I might have met with better accommodations. The Cuftom-houfe Officer
compelled the Ruffians, alfo, who had
brought me, to ftay with their horfes all
night, to conduct me the next day to Kotchim. My remonftrances on this head
were ineffectual, when oppofed to his intereft and convenience: He affected, indeed, to have no other motive than refpect
for me, and to have nothing but my convenience in view; when his only object
was, in fact, to fave an expence which muft
otherwife have fallen upon him.

In other refpects we could not perceive
that we put him to any expence, except
from the profufion with which we were
ferved; and the Pacha, whom he had acquainted with my arrival, increafed our
abundance by a prefent of flowers and fruit
he

he fent me, with the affurance of being well received, and better treated the next day.

The habit of living with the Turks rendered my evening, however, more tolerable than it would have been for any other perfon. I paffed a part of it in the Cuftom-houfe officer's kiofk, which was his ufual refidence ; and where, indolently ftretched out on the frontiers of defpotifm, in the full plenitude of his authority, this Turk exhibiting its genuine picture to the inhabitants of the oppofite fhore, was intoxicated with the pleafure of feeing nothing fo important as himfelf. He informed me, that two young Frenchmen had arrived a few days before at Kotchim, where, after taking the turban, they had fet out for Conftantinople. He fatisfied, alfo, my queftions refpecting the revenues of his Cuftom-houfe, which I found were as profitable to him, as they were burthenfome to thofe who had the misfortune to fall into his hands ; and as that was all the information to be got from him, I left him and went to take fome reft. The people, however, fent by the Pacha to conduct

duct me to Kotchim, and to receive me
there with diftinction, began to awaken
me from a found fleep at day break. Each
of them was eager to acquaint me with
the importance of his employment, in order to have a better claim on my genero-
fity. The people of the Cuftom-houfe
watched, alfo, the moment of my waking,
to come for their fhare. I rewarded the
guards too, who had attended me, and who
had been prevented from robbing me, only
by the particular attention of my fervants.
We then fet out with a pretty numerous
retinue, and I was foon fettled in the houfe
of a Jew, prepared for my reception in the
fuburbs of Kotchim.

An officer and fome Janiffaries, who
were to be my guard, occupied the gateway into which I was introduced by one of
the Governor's people, who had orders to
procure me, *gratis*, and at the expence of
the inhabitants, every neceflary. His firft
care, therefore, was to inquire what I
wifhed to be fupplied with. I was fhocked
at this fpecies of oppreflion, to which,
however, I was no ftranger ; but I knew
neither

neither the right, nor the refources of the oppreffors; I modeftly anfwered that I wanted nothing, and gave fecret orders to my own people to purchafe the neceffary provifions. I could not forefee that this was the very way to aggravate the oppreffion. A miferable Jew I had employed to make my purchafes, and who, in the hopes of cheating me, had overlooked the danger of his undertaking, was feized, baftinadoed, and forced to point out to my zealous purveyor, the people with whom he had been dealing, who efcaped, however, by returning the money, and with the lofs of their property. My broker difgorged alfo his profits, and the Turk gave back nothing; but he took fpecial care to order for the evening, and the next day, fuch a quantity of provifions, that he muft afterwards have fold, for his own account, a great part of them, which I could not poffibly confume.

Such fcenes greatly increafed my defire of haftening my arrival in the Crimea; but it was neceffary to obtain both the

Pacha's

Pacha's permiffion, and other affiftance
which he alone was able to procure me.
My firft care was to have an interview with
him as early as poffible ; for the Turks
are fo flow, and fo lazy themfelves, that
the firft civility they fhow to a ftranger is
to invite him to reft himfelf, and that was
the compliment I received on alighting;
but I affured them fo pofitively that nothing fatigued me fo much as repofe, that
I obtained an audience for the next day.
The Pacha, who lives in the fortrefs, fent
me horfes accordingly, at the hour appointed, and feveral of his officers to conduct me to him.

The fortrefs of Kotchim, fituated on
the rife of the mountain, on the right
border of the Niefter, hangs towards the
river, and lays the place entirely open to
the oppofite bank. The country of Poland, indeed, prefents this citadel with fo
delightful a profpect, that one would be
tempted to imagine that the Turkifh en-
gineers facrificed to that advantage, both
the defence and fafety of fo important a
port,

port, in which, as it now is, they would not be able to hold out three days againſt a regular attack.

The Pacha who commanded there was a venerable old man, with whoſe charac-ter I was in ſome meaſure already acquaint-ed. I knew that being naturally of a ti-mid diſpoſition, he feared that the Viſir had hoſtile intentions towards him, and I had reaſon to apprehend therefore, that he would not venture to let me paſs with-out an expreſs order from the Porte. He convinced me accordingly, after the firſt compliments were over, that I was not miſtaken, aſſuring me, however, that he would endeavour to make my ſtay agree-able ; but it was impoſſible to render any delay agreeable to me. I diſcuſſed the matter with him, therefore, and at length perſuaded him that he would run more riſk by detaining me at Kotchim, than by letting me paſs, ſince he would offend the Tartars, who were expecting me, without paying his court to the Viſir, who did not look for me, and the protection of the

Kam,

Kam, which I undertook to promife, over-
came his difficulties.   My departure was
fixed for the next day, and our parting was
the more friendly, as I made him underftand that my good offices might be of fervice to him.

His principal Tchoadar, who was to be
my Mikmandar†, came to wait on me at
my return home.   He concerted with me
the proper means to be taken, and then
left me to get his orders figned, and to prepare the poft-horfes for our journey. But
notwithftanding the alacrity with which
they feemed to fet to work to collect them,
we could not fet out until very late the
next day, and in fpite of the blows beftow-
ed on the unfortunate poftillions by my
Mikmandar, they went no fafter.   We
might have gone farther that day, however, had not Ali Aga, (that was the name
of my Mikmandar) made us ftop a league
fhort of the Pruth, to give himfelf time

† An officer appointed to go before Ambaffadors,
or other perfons, who travel by the order, and at the
expence of the Porte.

to

to prepare for the croffing of that river, for which purpofe he brought us to a tolerable good village, the miferable inhabitants of which were obliged to bring us provifions. A family foon turned out of doors, made room for us, and two fheep killed, roafted, and eaten, and not paid for, added to a few unneceffary blows, began to put me a little out of humour with my guide, who fet off in the evening to prepare every thing for the conveyance of my carriage over the Pruth.

I took the opportunity of his abfence, to give an old Turk, who appeared to be entrufted with the concerns of the community, the value of the provifions; but fome of the inhabitants prefently came to complain, that as I had not diftributed the fhares, they fhould not receive any part of the recompence I intended making them; " and," added they, " the old Turk to whom you have given all, is fupported by four cut-throat fons, who bear no part of our burthens, and yet always take poffeffion of the profits."

Thefe

Thefe poor wretches, whilft they were
making thefe complaints to me, never fuf-
pefted, certainly, that they had the good
fortune of living under an ariftocracy. To
fatisfy them, however, and to fulfil my original intentions, I doubled the fum, and
every one retiring to his place of reft,
I got into my carriage, where I fell into fo
found a fleep, that we were far advanced
on our way when I awoke. The Pruth was
only at a league's diftance, and my con-
duftor, whom we perceived on horfeback,
flogging up a troop of peafants he was in
the midft of, gave us to underftand that
we were not far from the river, on the
borders of which we arrived, without being fenfible of its proximity, from the
fteepnefs of its banks.

The Pruth feparates the Pachalick of
Kotchim from Moldavia. Ali-Aga had
fwam over to the oppofite fhore the night
before, and got together by dint of his
whip, near three hundred of the neighbouring Moldavians, and had employed them the
whole night in forming with the trunks

of

of trees an ill-contrived raft, on which he
had repaffed to our fide of the river; but
all that did not fatisfy me of its folidity.
I prepared myfelf, however, to facrifice,
if neceffary, my carriage, and every thing
upon it. I only fecured out of it my
pocket-book, fully determined not to expofe myfelf to fo evident a perfonal danger;
nor would I fuffer my own attendants to
go over, but referved them for a fecond
voyage, in cafe the firft fucceeded. Mean-
while, my conductor, proudly exulting at
having accomplifhed fo wonderful a work,
preffed me to get into my carriage.——
"How" faid I, vexed at his ftupidity,
" will you ever contrive to get it down to
the river?—How will you afterwards keep
it on your paltry raft, which is fcarce
large enough for it, and muft infallibly
fink under its weight?" "How?" faid
he, " why, with thefe two inftruments;"
fhewing me his whip, and upwards of a
hundred fturdy peafants he had brought
from the other fide: "Don't be uneafy;
I would make them bear the univerfe on
their

their fhoulders. And if the raft finks, thefe fellows can all fwim ; they fhall keep it up ; if you lofe the value of a pin, they fhall every one of them be hanged."

So much ignorance and barbarity fhock-ed me, without giving me more confidence in the raft. But my refolution was form-ed, I told him I would not go over with my attendants till the fecond trip, and therefore he might do as he thought pro-per. I fat down on the edge of a cliff, to take a better view of this great manœuvre, and to enjoy at leaft a fcene for which I expected to pay very dearly.

The fignal for the workmen to begin was then given, by pronouncing the name of God, followed by feveral fmacks of his whip. They undid the traces of my car-riage, and carried it in their arms to the brink of the precipice, where they had formed with their pickaxes a rough fort of fhelving, to facilitate its defcent ; but it was not without fhuddering, that I faw them on the point of being crufhed by the weight of my coach, which they got down however,

however, on the raft, where it could only be diagonally placed, and to keep it fteady in that pofition, four of thefe wretches were clapped under the wheels, the leaft motion of which would have carried the whole equipage to the bottom of the river. After this operation, which had made that part of the raft next the land fink into the mud, and had plunged it feven or eight inches deep under water on the other fide, they ftill had to work to get it afloat, which the hundred men at length effected. They then accompanied it, part of them wading and others fwimming, and guided it with long poles to the other fide, where fome buffaloes were in readinefs to draw up my carriage, which I faw in the twinkling of an eye on the top of the oppofite cliff. My fears were now at an end, and the raft returning, conveyed us over without a fha-dow of danger or difficulty.

It is eafy to imagine that Ali-Aga tri-umphed on the occafion, and on fetting out, I gave the value of a hundred and fifty livres, (fix or feven guineas) to the workmen ;

workmen; but what is not fo eafy to imagine, nor could I forefee it, that my conductor, attentive to all my actions, and to
every gefture, ftaid behind, to get his
portion of the trifling prefent I had made
thefe poor creatures.

In an hour afterwards he made his appearance, and immediately went on before
to prepare breakfaft, at three leagues from
the Pruth, where we came up with him,
whilft he was collecting provifions with the
fame inftrument with which he had con-
ftructed his rafts. Except the too frequent
ufe he made of his whip, Ali-Aga appeared to me to be a good humoured fellow,
and I undertook to make him in future
lefs lavifh of his blows.

The Baron.

Your dexterity in the paffage of the
Pruth, and the good cheer you provide for
us, my dear Ali-Aga, would be fully fa-
tisfactory, did you not beat thofe poor
Moldavians fo frequently, or if you only
beat them when they difobey you.

Ali-

Ali-Aga.

What fignifies it to them, whether it be before or after, fince they muft be beaten? Is it not better to do it at once than to lofe time?

Baron.

What do you mean by lofing time? Do you call that making a good ufe of it to beat, without reafon, a fet of poor creatures, whofe exertions, ftrength, and fubmiffion, perform wonders?

Ali-Aga.

What, Sir—you talk the Turkifh language—you have lived at Conftantinople —you know the Greeks; and you do not know that Moldavians will do nothing till you break their bones! You imagine then that your carriage would have croffed the Pruth if I had not beat them all night, and continued this difcipline until your arrival on the banks of the river?

Baron.

Yes; I think that the fear alone of being beaten would have made them do all this; but, however that may be, we have

no

no more rivers to pafs; the poft fupplies us with horfes, we want nothing but provifions, and that is my affair; for I will own to you, my dear Ali, that fuch as you procure for me by blows, are hard of digeftion; let me pay for them, that is all I defire.

Ali-Aga.

You certainly take the fureft way not to have an indigeftion; for your money will not even get you bread.

Baron.

Never fear; I'll pay them fo well that I fhall have the beft of every thing, and with more certainty than you could get it yourfelf.

Ali-Aga.

You will not have bread, I tell you; I know the Moldavians; they require beating; befides, I am ordered to defray your expences every where, and thefe rafcally infidels are rich enough to bear the heavieft charges; this is a trifling one, and provided we beat them, they will be contented.

Baron.

Baron.

Do not refuſe me, I beg of you, my dear Ali Aga ; I do not wiſh my expences to be defrayed, and I'll anſwer for it, they do not wiſh to be beaten, provided we pay them ; I take that upon myſelf—let me do as I think proper.

Ali-Aga.

But we ſhall die with hunger.

Baron.

At any rate, let us make a trial ; it is my fancy.

Ali-Aga.

Since you are determined, I conſent : Try your experiment, which appears ne-ceſſary to give you ſome idea of the Molda-vians ; but when you are better acquainted with them, remember that it is not right I ſhould go to bed without my ſupper ; and when your money and your rhetoric have both failed you, you will allow me, I hope, to make uſe of my method.

Baron.

Be it ſo ; and ſince we are agreed, I ſhall, when we arrive at the village where we

ſleep,

fleep, addrefs myfelf to the Primate‡, in
order to treat with him, in a friendly way,
for provifions, and a good fire, under fome
cover, where we may pafs the night without having any thing to do with the inhabitants, and be free from the danger of the
plague, which has juft broke out in Moldavia. " In this cafe, faid Ali-Aga, " I
need not go any farther," and he immediately ordered one of his people to follow
my directions, repeating, with a fmile,
that " he would not go to bed fupper-
lefs."

We did not arrive till after fun-fet at
the village where we intended to halt; and
we difcovered our lodgings by a fire they
had prepared for us.

My conductor, in order to keep to his
engagement with me, went to warm himfelf on alighting, and fat down with his
elbow leaning on his faddle, and his whip
in his hand, to enjoy the diverfion he ex-

‡ This title anfwers to that of Mayor; but his
functions differ in the fame proportion that flavery
differs from liberty.

pected

pected I fhould afford him. I was no lefs
defirous of procuring my provifions from
that fpirit which produces a mutual ex-
change of neceffaries. I inquired for the
Primate, whom they pointed out to me:
I went up to him, and prefenting him with
twenty crowns, (about two guineas and a
half,) which I laid upon the ground, fpoke
to him firft in Turkifh, then in Greek, in
thefe terms, faithfully tranflated :

The Baron. (In Turkifh.)

There, my friend, is money to buy the
provifions we fhall want. I have always
loved the Moldavians, and cannot bear they
fhould be ill treated. I hope you'll lofe
no time in procuring me a fheep §, and
fome bread ; keep the reft of the money
to drink my health.

The Moldavian. (Feigning not to
underftand Turkifh.)

He not underftand.

Baron.

What, don't you underftand Turkifh ?

_____

§ A fheep alive, ard of a good quality, is only
worth half a crown Eng'ifh.

The

The Moldavian.

No Turk; he not underſtand.

The Baron. (In Greek.)

Well, let us talk Greek then : Take this money, bring me a ſheep and bread; that is all I aſk of you.

The Moldavian. (Still feigning not to underſtand, and making ſigns to exprefs that there is nothing in his village, and that they are ſtarving.) Not bread; poor; he not underſtand.

Baron.

What have you no bread?

Moldavian.

No bread; no.

Baron.

Ah ! wretches, how I pity you; but at leaſt you ſhall not be beaten ; that is ſome conſolation. ·It is undoubtedly very hard to go to bed without any ſupper ; yet you are a proof that many honeſt men are obliged to do ſo. *(To the guide.)* You hear what they ſay, my dear Ali ; if money can get nothing here, you will own at leaſt that blows would have been ſuperfluous :

theſe

thefe poor creatures have nothing, and that grieves me more than having nothing ourfelves to eat for the prefent. We fhall have a better appetite to-morrow.

Ali-Aga.

For my part, it is impoffible to have a better appetite than I have to-day.

Baron.

It is your fault; why did you make us ftop in a poor village, where there is not even bread? You fhall faft for your punifh-ment.

Ali-Aga.

A poor village, Sir! A poor village! If the darknefs of the night did not prevent you from feeing, you would be delighted with it. It is a little burgh that abounds in every thing. One may find even cinna-mon § here.

Baron.

So, I fee that your defire of beating is returning upon you.

§ The Turks are very fond of this fpice, which they put in all their dilhes, and compare it to the moft exquifite delicacy.

Ali-Aga.

Ali-Aga.

No indeed, Sir; it is only my defire of fupping, which I certainly cannot get rid of; and to fatisfy it, and convince you that I am better acquainted with the Moldavians than you are, let me talk with him.

Baron.

Can you fatisfy your hunger by beating him?

Ali-Aga.

Yes, I'll anfwer for it; and if in a quarter of an hour you have not a moft excellent fupper, you may return me the blows I fhall give him.

Baron.

On this condition I confent, and take you at your word; but remember, that if you beat him without reafon, I fhall lay on you moft heartily.

Ali-Aga.

As long as you pleafe; but be as quiet a fpeƐtator as I have been during your negociation,

Baron.

Baron.

That is but fair ; I will take your place.

Ali-Aga. (Rifes, puts his whip under his coat, and advancing care-
lefsly towards the Greek, pats him
in a friendly way upon the fhoul-
der.)

Good day, friend ; how are you ? Well
——fpeak——don't you know Ali-Aga,
your friend ? Come ;——why don't you
fpeak ?

The Moldavian.

He not know.

Ali-Aga.

He not know!—Ah ! ah ! that is aftonifhing. What friend, ferioufly, you don't
underftand Turkifh ?

Moldavian.

No ; he not know.

Ali-Aga. (Knocks down the Primate
with his fift, and kicks him as he
is rifing.)

There, fcoundrel, that is to learn you
Turkifh.

Moldavian. (In good Turkiſh.)

Why do you beat me? Don't you know that we are poor people, and that our Princes hardly leave us the air we breathe in?

Ali-Aga.

Well, Sir; you ſee that I am a good language maſter; he already ſpeaks Turkiſh charmingly. We can now talk together at leaſt, that is ſomething. *(To the Moldavian, leaning on his ſhoulder.)* Now that you know a little Turkiſh, tell me how you and your wife and children all do?

Moldavian.

As well as people can do, who are often in want of the neceſſaries of life.

Ali-Aga.

You are facetious, my friend; you only want a little more beating; but all in good time; let us come to the point: I muſt have immediately two ſheep, twelve chick-ens, twelve pigeons, fifty pounds of bread, four oques * of butter, ſome ſalt, pepper,

* A Turkiſh weight, equal to about 42 ounces.

nutmegs,

nutmegs, cinnamon, lemons, wine, fal-
lad, and good oil of olives, and plenty of
each of them.

The Moldavian. (Crying.)

I have already told you we were poor
people who had not even bread, where
would you have us get cinnamon ?

Ali-Aga. (Pulling out his whip from
under his coat, and beating the
Moldavian till he runs away.)

Ah ! rafcally infidel, you have nothing!
I fhall take the fame method of enriching
you, that I did to learn you Turkifh.
*(The Greek runs away ; Ali-Aga returns
and fits by the fire.)* You fee, Sir, that
my receipt is better than yours.

Baron.

To make the dumb fpeak, I confefs ;
but not to get a fupper ; and I believe I
fhall have fome blows to give you, in your
turn, for your method does not procure
provifions any more than mine.

Ali-Aga.

Provifions ! Oh ! we fhall be in no want
of them : and if in a quarter of an hour,

all

all I have ordered be not here, take my
whip and return me all the blows I have
given him.

In fact, the quarter of an hour was not
expired before the Primate, affifted by
three of his countrymen, brought us all
the provifions, without forgetting the cinnamon.

After this example, it was impoffible to
deny the efficacy of Ali's receipt; and it
was fufficient to cure me of my obftinate
humanity. In fact, unaccountable as it
appeared, I was evidently wrong, and I
was compelled, though reluctantly, to
leave to my guide the care of fupplying
me with provifions in future, without difputing with him about the means.

The country through which we were
paffing, engaged all my attention. New
and picturefque fcenes, as interefting from
the luxuriant cultivation, as from the great
variety of objects, prefented themfelves at
every ftep; and I fhould compare Moldavia
with Burgundy, if the Greek principality
could

could enjoy the ineftimable advantages refulting from a moderate government.

Thefe people, who by the faith of trea-
ties have been long governed by their own
Princes, fhould to this day be no otherwife acquainted with defpotifm, than by
the change of their fovereigns at the will
of the Ottoman Porte. Moldavia and Wallachia were only fubject originally to a very
fmall tribute, and then enjoyed a fhadow
of liberty. They prefented in the perfons
of their princes, if not men of merit, at
leaft illuftrious names, refpected by the
conqueror, and the Greeks were ftill flattered to behold in thefe princes, the image
of their former mafters ; but every thing
was foon confounded ; the conquered
Greeks found themfelves no better than
flaves, and no longer admitted any diftinctions amongft them ; their mutual con-
tempt increafed their abafement, and in
this ftate of things, the Grand Signior
himfelf, no longer made any diftinction in
this defpicable herd. The merchant was
raifed to the principality—every adventu-

rer

rer thought himfelf intitled to that rank;
and thefe unhappy provinces, frequently
offered to the beft bidder, foon groaned
under the yoke of the moft cruel oppreffion.

An annual tax, become immoderate,
from the practice of felling the Principality to the higheft bidder, enormous fums
borrowed by the tributary, in order to purchafe the enfeofment, intereft at twenty-
five *per cent.* fums of money daily employed by others, to fruftrate the intrigues of
the pretenders, the luxury of thefe upftart
Princes, and the eager rapacioufnefs of
thefe ephemeral beings, are the caufes
which concur to lay wafte the two fineft
provinces of the Ottoman empire. If it
be confidered, that Moldavia and Wallachia are more burthened with taxes, and
more cruelly oppreffed, than they were in
their moft flourifhing ftate, it will be eafy
to form a juft idea of the deplorable fate of
thofe countries; as if the Defpot, folely
bent on deftruction, thought himfelf en-
titled to increafe his exactions in proportion

tion to the diminution of his people, and
the lofs of the fertility of their lands. I
was myfelf witnefs, in paffing through
Moldavia, to the levying of the eleventh
poll-tax in that year, though we were then
only in the month of October.

We now approached Yaffi, to which
place my guide had difpatched a meffenger, to announce my arrival. I had taken
the fame opportunity of fending compliments to the reigning Prince, who was fon
to the old Drogman of the Porte, of whom
I have already fpoken. I had reafon to
think our former acquaintance might be of
ufe to me in Moldavia; but I did not forefee that I fhould have a proof of his eagernefs to receive me, even before my arrival
in his capital. At a league's diftance, however, from that town, as we were ftrug-
gling in the dark, againft the difficulties
of a narrow fleep road, on a clay foil, I was
informed of the arrival of one of the Prince's
carriages which was fent to meet me. In
fact, it arrived juft in time to block up the
paffage ; and to complete my impatience,
a fecre-

a fecretary, who was fent to compliment
me, feeks me out in the dark, and acquits
himfelf fo tedioufly of his commiffion, that
I fhould have been there till now, had I
not confented to be removed into his ill-
contrived calafh, of which he wanted me
to admire the magnificence, in fpite of the
darknefs of the night. " Ah! my dear
Ali," cried I, " how excellent your receipt is!" For I faw, in fact, that Ali-
Aga, ever convinced of its efficacy, was at
that moment applying it with as much fuccefs as activity, to make them turn the
carriage in which I had taken my feat. I
tried to make the beft of my prefent fituation, by queftioning the fecretary on fuch
objects as had excited my curiofity, without endangering either his policy or his dif-
cretion; but in vain :—all I could get
from him were frefh affurances of his for-
row that the darknefs hindered me from
feeing the gilding of our car, and deprived
me of the fplendor of the triumphal entry
they had prepared for me.

We

We perceived, however, that we were entering the town, by means of a few fcattered lights, and the noife of planks, on which I found the carriage rolling, made me inquire of the fecretary the meaning of it. He informed me that thefe pieces of wood, laid near each other acrofs the ftreets, ferved to bear up the carriage, on account of the miry foil on which Yaffi was built. He added, that a fire had juft reduced the greateft part of the town to afhes; that they were then bufily employed in re-building it, but that the houfes would be built in a more modern tafte.—He was going to enter into particulars of the plans, when our carriage turning too fhort, and running againft the corner of the gateway, introduced us into the Convent of the Miffionaries, where I was to lodge, well pleafed at once to get rid of a very jumbling carriage, and moft difagreeable mafter of the ceremonies.

A tolerable good fupper was waiting for us, and fome Italian Cordeliers, fettled at Yaffi, under the King's protection, and the

direction

direction of the Society *de propaganda fide*, had prepared us convenient enough lodgings. Before I went to bed, I received a frefh compliment from the Prince on my fafe arrival, and on awakening had a vifit from the Governor. He was mounted on a horfe richly caparifoned ; a croud of fervants, dreffed like Tchoadars, accompanied this Greek, whom I had known at Conftantinople in a very inferior fituation. He feemed to be particularly defirous of exciting my admiration of the Oriental fplendor with which he was now furrounded, and I was, for my part, no lefs entertained at feeing him puffed up with the moft ridiculous pride. Ali-Aga, however, difconcerted every thing by his prefence. We have already feen that this Turk treated the Moldavians in the country with a great deal of levity, but I imagined he would lofe fomething of his importance and prerogative at Yaffi ; but in this I was again miftaken, for he foon made his appearance in a handfome drefs, with a grave carriage, and a tone of dignity. He played off,

off, in fhort, the courtier, who feeling that
he might one day be Vifir, and give Princes to Moldavia, already looked upon himfelf as their fuperior ; with this idea he
began with treating the Governor very in-
differently, for the negleft of the Grand
Equerry, who had not yet fent him the retinue which was to conduft him to the
Prince's audience. The Governor in vain
exculpated himfelf:—" You are all alike,"
replied Ali-Aga ; " but I will put matteis
in order." Fortunately the fo much wifhed for retinue arrived, which confifted in
a horfe neatly caparifoned, and four Tchoadars to accompany—Whom ? The Tchoadar of the Pacha of Kotchim, who was
himfelf only a Pacha of the fecond order.
But there are no gradations between a
Turk and a Greek ; the former is every
thing, and the latter—nothing.

It was on this unqueftionable principle
that Ali-Aga mounted his horfe with a fuperior majefty, and that every body he met
ftopped to make him a profound reve-
rence, which refpeftful homage he very
gravely

gravely returned by a flight nod of the
head and by a gracious fmile. His vifit
to the Prince produced him fome prefents,
and every ftep he took in Yaffi contributed
equally to his perfonal intereft and dignity.
Whilft my conductor was thus mixing the
utile dulci, I was contriving means to find
a fubftitute for him, that I might continue
my journey. The Prince could only undertake to fupply me to the Tartar frontiers ; I wrote therefore to the Sultan Serafker of Bafs-Arabia, requefting him to fend
to meet me on the confines of Moldavia.

My plan being thus laid, I got into one
of the Prince's carriages, in which, furrounded by a great many more equerries
and footmen than I wifhed for, I was conducted to the palace. I was anxious to get
in, to avoid the tedioufnefs of the Turkifh
ceremonies, which the Greek pride had
prepared for my reception.

I found the Prince alone with his brother, in an apartment, more remarkable
for two enormous arm chairs, covered with
fcarlet, than for its richnefs. I foon gueffed
                                          all

all their importance, but I conſtantly refuſed to take a ſeat on one of them. The
Prince himſelf then took another ſeat and
our former intimacy, which furniſhed matter for the beginning of our converſation,
induced him to truſt me with the hiſtory
of his preſent embarraſſing ſituation. I
eaſily perceived that the intriguing fana-
ticiſm of his brother, made it extremely
cruel, and expoſed him to very great
riſques in future. We terminated this
conference by concerting all the neceſſary
arrangements for my departure, after
which I was obliged to ſuffer all the
Turkiſh ceremonies. The moſt important, and which conveys the ſtrongeſt
mark of regard, is preſenting the ſherbet, which is always followed by ſprink-
ling you with roſe water, and perfume of
aloes. This ſherbet, ſo often ſpoken of in
Europe, and ſo little known there, is compoſed of cakes of preſerved fruits, diſſolved
in water, and ſo ſtrongly tinctured with
muſk, that one can ſcarcely taſte the liquor ; the ſame jar, therefore, once filled,
is

is fufficient for all the vifits of the week.
I took it cautioufly, as I did the fweetmeats
given with the coffee, and of which they
never change the fpoon. All this ceremonial, however, which was repeated for my
fervant in the anti-chamber, met with a
different, and not quite fo œconomical a
reception from him : his appetite refufed
nothing ; he eat all forts of preferved gin-
ger that were offered him ; he fwallowed,
at one draught, the whole jar of fherbet ;
and the courtiers were viewing him with
amazement, when I came out of the
Prince's apartment.

On my return to the Convent of the
Cordeliers, I found feveral Greeks of my
acquaintance waiting for me, fome of
whom I kept to dinner, and they afterwards accompanied me in the vifits I had
to return.

The town of Yaffi, fituated on a miry
foil, is furrounded by hills, on the fides of
which are the moft rural fpots, where delightful country houfes might be built ;
but where nothing is at prefent to be feen
but

but a few flocks; and excepting the houfes of the boyards, and thofe occupied by the Greeks, who came from Conftantinople in the Prince's fuite, to partake with him of the plunder of Moldavia, all the other dwelling houfes of the capital befpeak the greateft mifery.

The boyards * reprefent, with a great deal of ftatelinefs, the grandees of the country, but they are, in fact, no more than tolerable rich landholders, and very cruel oppreffors. It is rarely that they live on good terms with their Prince, and their intrigues are generally pointed againft him ; Conftantinople is the centre of their manœuvres. It is there that both parties carry their complaints, and their money, and the Sultan Serofkier, of Bafs-Arabia, affords a conftant refuge to fuch boyards as the Port is difpofed to facrifice to its tranquillity. The fafe-guard of the Tartar

* So the great landholders are called ; they are a fort of nobility without any other pretenfions than their wealth ; but every thing is in fubjection to riches, and the beft eftablifhed regulators with difficulty withftand them.

Prince

Prince enfures the impunity of the boyard ; his protection, not frequently, procures even his re-eftablifhment, but that
protection muft be paid for.

The different outgoings, for which
the boyards reimburfe themfelves by partial
perfecutions, joined to the taxes impofed
by the Prince to compleat his annual tribute, and the other articles of expence I
have already mentioned, opprefs Moldavia
to fuch a degree, that the richnefs of the
foil is fcarcely adequate to the purpofe. It
is alfo very certain that this, as well as
the neighbouring province of Wallachia, in
fubmitting to Mahomet II. with the claufe
of being refpectively governed by Greek
Princes, and of being fubject only to a moderate impoft, have not made fo good a
bargain as the framers of the treaty imagined ; undoubtedly, they did not forefee
that the vanity of the Greeks would expofe
thefe provinces to be put up to the beft
bidder : they muft have fhut their eyes,
too, againft the claufe referved to the
Grand Signior of removing them at pleafure.

fure. A terrible bargain this, between a greedy defpot, and thefe haughty flaves, whom he can exalt to a Principality when he thinks proper, and ftrip them of it by a nod ! It is evident that this power of removal could not fail of carrying the annual tribute of thefe provinces, by a rapid progreffion to an exceffive height, and that a general fyftem of depredation muft be the neceffary confequence; and accordingly, the whole art of thefe fubordinate governments confift in embracing, and employing every poffible means of accelerating this horrid fcene of plunder.

Moldavia and Wallachia were an ancient Roman colony. A corrupted Latin is fpoken there to this day, and this language is called *Roumié*, the Roman tongue. Thefe provinces, wretched enough under the lofty yoke of the Romans, groan at prefent under the weight of a more cruel, and more humiliating oppreffion—they are pillaged by a fet of fubalterns, vefted with a momentary and precarious authority.

Every

Every thing being ready for continuing
my journey, I quitted Ali-Aga after rewarding him for his good offices, and left
Yaffi, attended by two Janiffaries of the
Prince's guard, and a Greek, who was
to be my conductor. This triumvirate,
wherever we came, purfued the great principles fo happily adapted to the Moldavian manners, and which Ali-Aga had
taught me; but a ftriking inftance of violence and robbery exhibited by the Turks,
deferves to be recorded. We were paffing
through a pretty enough valley, with hills
on each fide, where fome fheep were feed-
ing under the care of feveral fhepherds:
happening to afk one of the Janiffaries
fome queftions refpecting the quality of
the wool in that country; "You fhall
judge of that very foon," fays he; he then
fpurs his horfe up towards the flock, dif-
perfes it, wheels about in the midft of it,
fixes on the largeft fheep, rides after, and
comes up with it in a gallop; ftoops down,
feizes it by the fleece, lifts it with one
hand, places it before him on the faddle,

recovering

recovering his feat himfelf, and comes up
to me full fpeed. I made feveral fruitlefs
efforts to make him reftore the animal to
the owner, or to pay him the value of it.
They laughed at my delicacy; the Turk
kept the prize, on which he and his comrades regaled themfelves in the evening.

This part of Moldavia appeared to me as
beautiful as the country we had paffed
through to arrive at Yaffi; but it became
more mountainous as we approached Kiche-
now. We defcended, at length, through defiles, which becoming longer, and opening
out more as we advanced, we difcovered
from their bottom the country of Bafs
Arabia. We had fcarce entered it before
we faw the declivities to right and left
covered with dromedaries †. The Greek
I had

---

† This animal, which has two large lumps on his
back, is much larger than the camel, who has only
one; but it feems that naturalifts are not generally
agreed on the fubject of the names which ought to
diftinguifh thefe two fpecies of animals. As the
Arabs, however, who have only the camel with one
lump, call him dévé, or l'aûtréche duvé couchou, the
bird,

I had with me obferved, that thefe animals, which belong to the Tartars, by thus en- croaching on a foreign territory, fre- quently give rife to difputes, which never terminate until the pafturage in litigation is eaten up. We foon faw a greater number of thefe herds, and I remarked amongft them fome white dromedaries.

We had fcarcely paffed the frontier be- fore we perceived a troop of horfemen coming towards us. It was the interpre- ter of the Sultan Serafker, fent by that Prince to meet me, with ten fcimens of his guard. My meffenger whom I had difpatched from Yaffi, was likewife with them. He delivered me the Sultan's an- fwer, and the interpreter added the com- pliment he was ordered perfonally to make me ; after which four horfemen arrang- ing themfelves as a van guard, we conti- nued our journey through a flat country,

bird, or oftrich camel It feems proper to diftinguifh by the name dromedary, fuch animals of the fame genus, as have two lumps.

entirely

entirely open, and on a hard foil, where the print of the road was fcarcely vifibie.

My new conductor was a renegado Jew, born in Poland ; he fpoke German, and was fo loquacious, that I had no occafion to afk him any queftions, to get at the bottom of his whole hiftory. He informed me, alfo, that the Noguais were difcontented with the Kam, who had been fo weak as to transfer to the Grand Signior the duty of Ichetirach *, in the two provinces of Yedefan and Dgamboylouk, through which I muft pafs in my way to Orcapi ; but our converfation was frequently interrupted by a circumftance not deferving of mention, had it not ferved to give the fuperftitious Tartars a favourable opinion of me.

On my arrival on the frontier, where I was met by my efcort, a ftork, a bird which feeds on ferpents, and builds on houfes, and is held in veneration by the eaftern nations, as a fort of houfhold God,

* I have already faid that this duty was paid in corn, at a very unfair price for the hufbandmen.

feemed

feemed alfo to come on purpofe to meet
me; it flies paft fwiftly to the left, very
near my carriage; flies round it, repaffes
on the right, purfues its flight by the high-
way, and fits down at twelve hundred feet
diftance before the horfemen, who preceded
me; rifes when they come near, refumes
its flight towards my carriage, again makes
the circuit, goes and takes its advanced poft
as before, and repeats this manœuvre until
our arrival at Kichela †.

This town, the refidence of the Sultan
who commands at Bafs Arabia, is confidered as the capital of that province. The
Prince who filled this ftation was the eldeft
fon of the reigning Sultan, and had the
title of Serafker ‡, (Generaliffimo). A
Mirza § on my arrival came to compli-

† Kichela means winter quarter.

‡ Serafker, a Turkifh word compofed of SER,
which in Perfian means Head, and of ASKER, Sol-
diers; it is a military rank which admits of no fuperior; it can only be compared with Generaliffimo,
and that title is ufually given to thofe who command
on the frontier, or who are detached with a confiderable body of troops.

§ Mirza, the title of all the nobles. The reader
will find in the courfe of thefe Memoirs, the different
claffes of the Tartar nobility.

ment

ment me on his part, and to conduct me to the lodgings prepared for me. I went immediately with this gentleman to wait upon the Sultan ‡. He was a young Prince, of eighteen or twenty years old, of a good fize, well made, with a countenance more noble than agreeable, and whofe modeft demeanour occafioned a little embarraffment, which I took care to remove; and I difcovered that this Prince, as well as the Mirzas who compofed this pretended barbarous Court, were poffeffed of infinitely more foftnefs and amenity, than are found very frequently amongft thofe who are called polifhed nations.

Excepting the dreffes of the Sultan, and the Mirzas, which, without being rich, are diftinguifhed by a fort of luxury and elegance, the furniture amongft the Tartars is confined to what is ftriftly neceffary. The luxury of window glafs is no where to be feen but in the Prince's apartments; paper frames are the only windows made

‡ We have already feen that Sultan means a Prince of the blood.

ufe

ufe of in other houfes during the winter,
which they remove in fummer to breathe
more freely, and to enjoy, without ob-
ftruction, the diftant profpect of the Black
Sea. The Sultan entertained me at fupper ; and notwithftanding I had a very
great appetite, it did not efcape me that
the excellent fifh of the Niefter deferved
better cooks than are to be found amongft
the Tartars. Hawking, and grey-hound
courfing, feemed to me to be their only
amufement ; and the Sultan made thefe
parties very frequently with a numerous
retinue of Mirzas. They fet out on thefe
hunting parties, which laft feveral days,
with arms and baggage ; the camp is
formed every evening ; a body of troops
always makes part of the Serafker's retinue, and fometimes thefe parties of pleafure are only a pretext for more ferious
expeditions.

The night was paffed in repairing a little carriage I had bought at Yaffi, and
which I had converted into a *dormeufe*, (or
carriage for fleeping in ;) a waggon carried
the

the baggage which had been faſtened to
my carriage all the way from Moldavia ;
and the Sultan's orders being forwarded, I
ſet off the next day from Kichela with a
Mirza, who had orders to conduct me to
Bactcheſeray §, eſcorted by forty horſemen
armed with bows and arrows, and with
ſabres. Accuſtomed to the want of order,
diſcipline, and military knowledge which
reigns amongſt the Turkiſh troops, I had
no reaſon to ſuppoſe the Tartars were any
better. After paſſing the Nieſter, however, which ſeparates Baſs Arabia from
Yedeſan, where there was ſuppoſed to be
a ſort of inſurrection amongſt the herds, the
officer who commanded the detachment

§ Bactcheſeray is the reſidence of the Kani of the
Tartars. This town, at preſent conſidered as the capital of the Crimea, was formerly nothing but a country houſe, called the Palace of the Gardens. The ſo-
vereigns by living there have drawn together a number of inhabitants; and this town ſtill keeping the
ſame name, has ſucceſſively uſurped the pre-eminence
over the ancient town of Crimea, which is now no
more than a paltry village, where the tombs alone
teſtify its ancient importance.

diſpoſed

difpofed the order of march like an enlightened foldier: a van guard of twelve
horfemen preceded my carriage at two hundred paces diftance, which the officer took
under his particular protection, with eight
men, four of whom were placed on each
fide; two waggons followed after, eight
other horfemen clofed the march, and two
little platoons, of fix men each, at more
than fix hundred paces diftance, kept a
look out to the right and left.

The plains we croffed were fo level
and open, that the horizon appeared only
a hundred paces from us on every fide. No
rifing ground, not even the fmalleft fhrub
to make a variety in this picture; and we
perceived nothing during the whole journey, but a few Noguais on horfeback,
whofe heads were difcovered by the piercing eyes of my Tartars, when the convex-
ity of the earth ftill hid the remainder of
their bodies. Each of thefe Noguais was
riding alone on horfeback, and thofe who
were queftioned by our patroles, made us
eafy on the fubject of the pretended troubles

bles we had been told of. I was curious to know, what could be the object of thefe men, and was informed, thefe people thought to be Nomades, becaufe they live in a fort of tents, were fettled in tribes, in vallies of fifty or fixty feet deep, which interfect the plain from north to fouth, and are more than thirty leagues in length, by half a quarter of a league in breadth, the middle of which are occupied by fome muddy rivulets, and terminate towards the fouth by fmall lakes that communicate with the Black Sea ‡. The tents of the Noguais are on the banks of thefe rivulets,

‡ Notwithftanding the barren appearance of the whole Tartar country, and facility with which they may compare their foil with that of the Moldavians, and Poles, to enable them to form a judgment of the advantages poffeffed by the latter, habit has fuch an empire over us, and the wants of men are relatively fo connected with this habit, that it gets the better of every fenfation. The Noguais have an idea that it is impoffible to crofs their plains without envying them their poffeffion. " You have travelled a great deal," faid one of the Tartars to me, with whom I was pretty intimate, " Did you ever fee fo rich a country as ours?" It is evident that this epithet, once eftablifhed, admitted of no contradiction.

as well as the hovels to fhelter the numerous flocks of this paftoral people during
the winter. Every proprietor has his particular mark, which is made with a hot
iron on the thigh of the horfes, oxen, and
dromedaries; the fheep, marked with colour on the fleece, are kept in fight, and
ftray very little from the habitations; but
all the other kinds, collected in particular
herds, are driven in the fpring to the plains,
where the proprietor abandons them till
winter.   At the approach of that feafon
he goes in fearch of them, to bring them
back under his hovels.   This was the employment of the Noguais we met with;
but it is very remarkable, that a fingle
Tartar thus employed in an extent of plain
which is never lefs than from ten to
twelve leagues wide, by more than thirty
leagues in length, from one valley to the
other, is ignorant even on what fide to
bend his fteps, nor does he reflect about
it.   He puts thirty days provifions, confifting of millet flour roafted, in a little
bag; fix pounds of flour are enough for
his

his confumption. His provifions made, he mounts his horfe, never ftops till fun fet, puts fhackles on his horfe, leaves him to graze, fups on his flour, goes to fleep, and awakening in the morning, continues his journey. In his way, however, he obferves the mark of the herds he meets with, retains them in his memory, communicates his difcoveries to the different Noguais employed in the fame bufinefs, tells them what he is looking after, and in return receives fuch ufeful informations as terminate his expedition. It is undoubtedly to be feared, that fo patient a people, endowed with fuch qualities, may one day furnifh a very formidable military force.

Our firft day's journey was to the neareft valley, which was only at ten leagues diftance. The fun, however, was on the decline, and I faw nothing before me but a melancholy horizon, when on a fudden I felt my carriage on the defcent, and I perceived the row of Obas †, which ex-

† Obas; the tents of the Noguais.

tended

tended along the valley, to right and left, as far as the eye could reach. We croffed the rivulet on a little bridge, near which I found three of thefe Obas out of the line, and one of them, entirely new, defigned for me. My carriages were placed behind it; the detachment ftaid near me. My firft care was to examine the whole of the picture, of which my retinue formed a detached groupe. Above all, I remarked that folitude in which we were left, and which aftonifhed me the more, as I thought myfelf an object fufficiently curious to merit fome attention. The Mirza had quitted me on our arrival, to look after provifions, and I employed myfelf, in the mean time, in examining the ftructure of my Tartar houfe. It was like a large poultry bafket, built in lattice work, and formed in a circular inclofure, over which was a dome, open at the top; a felt of camel's hair co-vered the whole on the outfide, and the hole at the top, intended occafionally as a vent-hole for the fmoke. I obferved, alfo, that the Obas inhabited by the Tartars, and

in

in which they made fires, had each of
them a fimilar piece of felt, tied in the
fhape of a flag, in the oppofite direction
from the wind, and fupported by a long
ftick from the infide of the Obas. The
fame ftick was made ufe of to let down
this fort of fan, when on extinguifhing
the fire, the aperture was become ufelefs
or inconvenient.

I particularly admired the folidity, united with the delicacy of the lattice work;
pieces of raw leather are ufed for faftening
them together; and I underftood that my
Obas, defigned for a new married woman,
made part of her dowry.

We had very great appetites, and with
much fatisfaction faw the Mirza return
with two fheep, and a kettle he had procured. The kettle was fufpended to
three fticks, feparated at the bottom, and
joined at the top. The kitchen thus ar-
ranged, the Mirza, the officer, and fome
Tartars, proceeded to kill and cut up the
fheep, with which they filled the pot,
whilft others were preparing fpits to roaft
what

what it could not contain. I had taken care
to make a provifion of bread at Kichela.
This is a luxury with which the Noguais
are unacquainted, and their avarice hin-
ders them from making an habitual ufe of
flefh meat, which however they are very
fond of. I was curious to know what way
they cooked, and to tafte their victuals, as
well as the good cheer which was preparing for me. The Mirza, to whom I communicated my whim, fmiled at it, and difpatched a Tartar, with orders to collect
every thing which could fatisfy my curiofity. He foon returned with a jar full of
mare's milk, a little bag of flour of millet
roafted, fome fmall white balls of the fize
of an egg, and as hard as chalk, an iron
pot, and a young Noguais, tolerably well
clad, and the beft cook of the hord. I
paid all poffible attention to his manner of
proceeding.—He fills his pot three quarters full of water, about four quarts, to
which he adds about fix ounces of the
roafted millet flour ; he places his jar
near the fire, pulls out a flat knife, wipes
it

it on his sleeve, stirs the contents about in a circular direction, always the same way, until the first simmering of the liquor; he then asks for one of the white balls, which was cheese, made of mare's milk, saturated with salt, and dried; breaks it in small pieces, throws it into his ragout, contriving to stir it round in the same direction; the contents begin to thicken, and he still keeps stirring, but with difficulty at last, until the whole was of the consistence of bread without yeast; he then draws out his flat knife, empties the kettle on his hand, and presents me with a cylinder of puff-paste in a spiral form. I was anxious to taste it, and was really better pleased with the mess than I expected. I tasted also the mare's milk, which perhaps I should likewise have found good, but for a sort of prepossession I could not overcome.

Whilst I was employed with so much luxury about my supper, a more interesting scene was preparing for me.

I have already said, that on my arrival, the Noguais retired each of them to his

hut,

hut, fhewing no curiofity to fee me, and
I had already made a facrifice of my vanity
on that head, when I perceived a confiderable troop of them advancing towards us;
the tranquillity, the flownefs even with
which they approached, could give us no
uneafinefs. We could not, however, conceive the motives which brought thefe Noguais on our fide, until we faw them ftop
at the diftance of four hundred paces, and
one of them advancing alone till he came
near the Mirza who conducted me, communicated to him the defire the chiefs of
his nation had to fee us; adding, that un-
willing, in the fmalleft degree, to difturb
our reft, he was deputed to inquire if their
curiofity would not difpleafe me ; and in
cafe it fhould not, which would be the
place where his companions would the leaft
incommode me? I anfwered the ambaffador myfelf, and affured him that they were
all at liberty to mix with us; that amongft
friends there was no diftinction of place,
much lefs any particular line of feparation.
The Noguais infifted on the orders he had
in

in that refpect, and the Mirza rofe up to
point out to him the fpot to which the
fpectators might advance, which was foon
occupied by this curious troop. I approached alfo, to take a nearer view of
them, and to have the pleafure of making
acquaintance with thefe gentlemen. They
all rofe upon my coming within reach,
and the moft remarkable amongft them, to
whom I addreffed myfelf, faluted me, by
taking off his cap, and making an inclina-
tion of his body. I obferved that the de-
puty had ufed the fame ceremonial to the
Mirza, which furprized me the more as
the Turks never uncover their heads,
but to be more at their eafe, and that
only when they are alone, or amongft
very familiar friends. It is for this reafon
alfo, that the European Ambaffadors, and
their retinue, go to the Grand Signior's
audience with their hats on, and it would
be a breach of decorum to prefent onefelf
otherwife before a Turk; but I fhall have
fome more important remarks to make on
the refemblance between our cuftoms and
thofe of the Tartars.

If

If I derived little information from my
Noguais, it was undoubtedly becaufe I neglected to afk fuch queftions as might have
enlightened me. The natural fondnefs we
have for novelty, however, rendered the
clofe of this day tolerably agreeable. I did
very well too with my fupper; but the
Tartar cookery owed its fuccefs amongft
my attendants only to their good appetite,
which gave a relifh to every thing. They
had no idea that one could fometimes take
a pleafure in indifferent entertainment. It
was apparently on my account only that
they complained; but I have fince been
perfectly well convinced, that the fole intereft they took in my perfonal comfort,
was only to give them the right of lament-
ing freely their own privations; by parta-
king of their wants, I difcovered the method of rendering my fervants lefs trouble-
fome; and I give this as the beft poffible
receipt to all travellers.

However interefting thefe Noguais were,
defirous of fhortening my ftay amongft
them, and of going the next day to the fecond

cond valley, I fet out early in the morning, and we faw the fun appear on the horizon of thefe plains as mariners obferve him on the ocean. We difcovered nothing this morning but fome little hillocks, like thofe one fees in many parts of Flanders *, and particularly in Brabant, where the common opinion is, that they have been formed by the hands of men, and by the combination of fhovels full of earth, brought by each foldier in antient times, to throw on his General's corpfe, by way of maufoleum. A great number of thefe hillocks, are likewife to be feen in Thrace, where, as well as in Tartary, in Brabant, and in every place where they are to be found, they are never fingle. But the quantity of thefe peculiar accumulations, difpofed, as they generally are, at almoft equal diftances, and always with a conformity of pofition which feems to befpeak defign, more than the fimple effect of hazard, led me to trace out, from the

* They are to be found in various parts of England; near Steverage, in Hertfordfhire, &c. and are known likewife by the name of Butts.

cuftoms

cuftoms now in ufe, the origin of thefe
pretended maufoleums. It appears to me,
that their origin may be difcovered in the
cuftom prevailing at this day amongft the
Turks, when they go to war, of marking
by hillocks of earth, placed in fight of one
another, the route to be followed by their
army. Thefe elevations, it is true, are
not fo high as thofe I have juft been fpeak-
ing of, and which have refifted the operation of ages on the furface of the earth.—
But may it not be added to my obfervation, that even if the hillocks of the an-
cients had no other object than to mark
out the march of their armies, in order to
infure their communication, the fpirit of
conqueft, which made them penetrate into
unknown countries, would naturally in-
duce them to preferve thefe points of information from too eafy a deftruction.—
With refpect to the bones which have been
found under fome of thefe hillocks, they
only prove, that they were *alfo* made ufe
of as burial-places for their generals and
foldiers, who died on the march. But the
greateft part of the butts which have been
under-

undermined in Flanders, prove that *all*
thefe heaps were not places of fepulture;
and if we recur to the idea of confidering
them as marks, this hypothefis will give
the further explanation of the works fpoken of by Xenophon, in his Retreat of the
Ten Thoufand. An unknown foil muft
every inftant have prefented obftacles to
the Greeks, more difficult to furmount,
and fnares more formidable, than the nations themfelves who were to be intimida-
ted or repelled.

On my journey I faw no appearance of
agriculture; becaufe if the Noguais fowed
their corn in frequented places, near the
high-roads, their corn would only ferve
for pafturage for travellers horfes. But if
thefe precautions preferve the Tartars from
this fpecies of depredation, nothing can
fave their fields from a more fatal calamity. Clouds of locufts, that frequently
fhower down on the plains of the Noguais,
choofe in preference the fields of millet,
and deftroy them in an inftant. The horizon is darkened by their approach, and
the

the cloud produced by the prodigious multitude of thefe animals, obfcures the fun.
If the Noguais hufbandmen happen to be
fufficiently numerous, they fometimes fucceed by their geftures, and their cries, in
averting the ftorm ; if not, the locufts
alight on their fields, and form a bed of
ſix or ſeven inches thicknefs. To the noife
of their flight, fucceeds that of their de-
vouring labour, which refembles the clat-
tering of hail, and the confequences are
more deſtructive. Fire itfelf is not more
active ; and not a trace of vegetation is to
be diſcovered when the cloud has refumed
its flight, to produce freſh difafters in other
places.

This calamity would extend itfelf, no
doubt, to countries where the culture is
more abundant, and Greece, and Afia
Minor, would be more frequently expofed to it, did not the Black Sea ſwallow
up the greateſt part of thefe clouds of
locuſts when they attempt to pafs that
barrier.

I have often feen the fhores of the Pon-
tus Euxine, towards the Thracian Bofphorus,

rus, covered with their dried carcaffes, and in fuch numbers, that it was impoffible to walk on the fhore without finking half-leg deep into this bed of their fkinned fkeletons. Curious to know the real caufe of their deftruftion, I have fought for opportunities to obferve the moment of it, and I have been witnefs to their total deftruction by a ftorm, which furprized them fo near the coaft, that their bodies were floated thither by the waves before they were dry; their carcaffes produced fuch an infectious fmell, that it was many days before one could come near them.

We arrived at the fecond valley before noon; and whilft the Mirza who condufted me, was fearching for the perfons who were to order the neceffary relays of horfes, I went up to a groupe of Noguais collefted round a dead horfe, which they had juft been fkinning. A young man naked, of about eighteen years old, received on his fhoulders the fkin of the animal. A woman, who performed the office of taylor, began by cutting the back of this new coat,

coat, following with her fciffars the fhape
of the neck, the fall of the fhoulders, the
femi-circle which joins the fleeve, and the
fide of the habit, which came down below
the knee. It was unneceffary to fupport a
ftuff, which, from its humidity, already
adhered to the fkin of the young man. The
woman taylor proceeded very fmartly to
form the crofs lapels and the fleeves, after
which the mannikin, who ferved as a mold,
fitting down fquat, gave her the opportunity of ftitching the pieces together ; fo
that cloathed in lefs than two hours in an
excellent *brown bay* coat, nothing remained for him but to tan this leather by conftant exercife, which was accordingly the
firft thing he did, and I faw him prefently
mount a horfe bare-backed, to join his
comrades, who were employed in collecting the horfes I wanted, the number of
which was not nearly compleated.

We already know that the Tartar horfes
are difperfed over the plains, in particular
droves, and diftinguifhed by the mark of
the proprietor; but as there are occafions
when

when each individual muſt contribute to
the public ſervice, there is alſo a particular drove of horſes for that purpoſe, belonging to the whole community.   This
drove is kept near, and within ſight of their
dwellings ; but theſe animals at liberty, in
an open country, are not eaſily got hold of;
it is evident, likewiſe, that the choice which
muſt neceſſarily be made of different horſes, for draught and for the ſaddle, increa-
ſes the difficulty.   The Noguais ſucceed in
this by a method which furniſhes the
young men deſtined for that ſort of hunting, with the opportunity of becoming the
moſt intrepid, and moſt ſkilful horſemen
in the world.   For this purpoſe they provide themſelves with a long pole, at the
end of which is faſtened a cord, the extremity of which terminated in an eye-let,
paſſed through the pole, forms a running
knot, open enough eaſily to admit a horſe's
head.   Furniſhed with this implement,
theſe young Noguais, mounted on horſes
bare-backed, the longe of the halter paſſed
through the horſe's mouth, ride up to the
drove

drove full gallop, obferve the animal which fuits them, follow him with extreme agility, come up with him, notwithftanding his fhifts, to which they accommodate themfelves with wonderful addrefs, gain on him by fwiftnefs, and feizing the moment that the end of the pole reaches beyond the horfe's ears, they flip the running knot over his head, flacken their fpeed, and thus retain their prifoner, whom they conduct to their depofitory.

As I was in want of near eighty horfes, and there were only half a dozen horfemen in purfuit of them, their exercife lafted long enough to give me all the pleafure of it ; but the relays were fo well chofen, that we were able to arrive in pretty good time in the fuburbs of Oczakow where we lodged.

This fortrefs, fituated on the right bank of the Boriftenes, and near its mouth, is built on a fmall declivity which goes down to the river. A ditch, and a covered way, are the only works for the defence of the place ; it is in the fhape of a parallel-
logram,

logram, bending on its length ; and one
obferves there, as well as at Bender, and
at Kotchim, a numerous artillery, every
piece of which, badly mounted, is bound
together by two enormous gabions, which
ferving by way of parapet, form the em-
brafures of the fortification.

Some Jews fettled there, keep inns in
the fuburbs of Oczakow. They were of
great fervice to us in renewing our provifions, and enabling us to crofs the plains
of Dgamboylouk, inhabited alfo by the
Noguais. The morning of the next day
was taken up in paffing the Boriftenes.
This river, ftrengthened towards its mouth
by a tongue of land belonging to the oppofite bank, and which is called Kilbourns †,
or Kilburn, forms within it a fort of lake,
which ftretches northward, from whence
the river flows. It is more than two leagues
broad between Oczakow and the fort oppofite, which is fituated at the end of the
point of land. It was in this direction that
we paffed the Boriftenes. Sailing veffels

† The nofe, or promontory of the hair.

are

are built for the purpofe, which take the opportunity of a favourable wind, and may alfo be pufhed with poles from its fhallow-nefs, every where but in the middle, where it is deep only for a few yards.

After three hours of this tedious naviga-tion, during which we had nothing to en-tertain us but the leaping of a few dolphins, we landed at Kilbourns, oppofite to the caftle which is built there. The landing of my carriages, and the collecting of the horfes we had occafion for, took up the conductors the reft of the day, which I employed in vifiting the caftle, where I found nothing remarkable but its inutility. Its artillery, in fact, defigned to co-operate with that of Oczakow, in the defence of the river, unable to form a crofs fire at fo great a diflance, leaves the paffage up the middle unmolefted. But I could not help remarking, that batteries placed on the point of Kilbourns, and upon a ledge of rock, fituated on the oppofite bank, would always prevent the entrance of every fort of veffel; this the Turks have never yet been

been able to calculate, and I fhall have other more important occafions of fixing the limits of their military knowledge.

We agreed to fet out an hour before daylight, and I made choice of a waggon prepared for me to fleep in, that I might take fome reft, of which I began to be very much in want.

The commander of my efcort knew nothing of this arrangement, and after diftributing his troops in the order I have already explained, he very affiduoufly follows my coach till he difcovered, by the day-light, that I was not in it ; he then complained very heavily of their negligence in not pointing out to him the carriage I was in, and immediately furrounded it with the little band he had referved for that purpofe. The reader will doubtlefs perceive, that I only relate this circumftance from its developing the character of the Tartars, which invariably exhibits the feeds of the moft correct ideas.

The road we took brought us near the Black Sea, and in following the beach from time

time to time, the very noife of the waves
afforded us a more interefting object, than
we could find in the naked plains over
which we had been paffing.   Thofe we
ftill had to pafs, were likewife entirely
bare, although I have been affured, that
they were formerly covered with forefts,
and that the Noguais had torn up even the
fmalleft ftumps, to avoid all poffibility of
a furprize.   But if this precaution effectu-
ally fecures a nation fo tranfportable as to
move off with every thing in lefs than two
hours, it deprives the Tartars of the fuel
which is fo neceffary in that climate.   To
provide againft this want, each family carefully collects the dung of the cattle, which
they knead with a fort of fandy earth, and
produce a turf which unfortunately fmokes
the Tartars more than it warms them.

No people live more foberly. Millet and
mares milk are their ufual diet.   The Tartars, however, are very carniverous.   A
Noguais might lay a wager that he eat a
whole fheep, and win his wager, without
having an indigeftion.   But their tafte in
this

this refpe&t is reftrained by their avarice ;
and that avarice is carried to fuch a length,
that, in general, they retrench every article
of confumption of which they can difpofe.
It is only, therefore, when one of their animals is accidentally killed, that they regale themfelves with its flefh ; but never
unlefs they arrive in time to bleed the dead
animal. They obferve the precepts of Mahomet, alfo, with refpe&t to fick animals.
The Noguais watch all the periods of the
diforder, in order to feize the moment,
when, finding their avarice condemned to
lofe the value of the animal, they may at
leaft gratify their appetite, by flaying it a
moment before its natural death.

The fairs of Balta, and fome others on
the frontiers of the Noguais country, procure them a fale for the immenfe droves
they are poffeffed of. The grain, which
they colle&t in abundance, finds a vent
likewife by the Black Sea, as well as wool
in general, and that kind called *pelades* § :

§ That wool is called pelades, which is feparated
from the fkin by means of lime. This operation cannot take place on living animals. It procures the
greateft quantity of wool, but injures the quality.

to thefe articles of commerce muft be added fome bad leather, and a great quantity of hare fkins.

Thefe different articles combined, procure the Tartars very confiderable annual
returns, which they will only receive in
Dutch or Venetian ducats ; but the ufe
they make of them deftroys every idea we
might be led to form of their wealth from
this prodigious quantity of fpecie.

Perpetually accumulating, and no part
of it returning into circulation by any kind
of barter, avarice takes poffeffion of, and
buries all the riches, and the plains they
are concealed in, offer not a trace to aid
thofe refearches which they otherwife
might tempt. Several Noguais dying without communicating their fecret, have already deprived the world of confiderable fums.
It is alfo to be prefumed, that thefe people
are perfuaded, that if they were forced to
abandon their country, they might fafely
leave their money without forfeiting their
property ; and, in fact, it would be of the
fame ufe to them five hundred leagues
diftance.

diftance. They derive no other enjoyment from it than the mere pleafure of poffef- fion ; but this has fo many attractions for them, that a Tartar frequently takes a thing for the fole pleafure of poffeffing it a moment : compelled foon after to reftore it, he muft pay likewife a confiderable pe- nalty ; but he has enjoyed it in his way, and he is contented. The avidity of the Tartars never calculates eventual loffes. They are fatisfied with the enjoyment of momentary advantages.

We now approached Orcapi, and had only one bad night's accommodations to fuffer, when I received a meffenger who was fent to meet me. He was commif- fioned by the Kam of the Tartars to en- fure me thofe conveniencies which I had already been fortunate enough to procure myfelf.

We paffed the night in a wretched ho- vel, covered with reeds, the only produce of the marfh in which it was fituated, near the fea. We travelled next morning along the beach, and foon came in fight of the

E 2   weftern

weſtern ſide of the peninſula, which ſtretched into the ſea on our right-hand. This
land, which was likewiſe flat, but more elevated than the plain we were on, was joined to it by ſo gentle a ſlope, as if it had been
formed by the line, and the upper part of
it preſented us with the profile of the lines
of Orcapi. We travelled by the ſide of
them pretty early in the morning, and
paſſed the ditch on a bad wooden bridge,
which joins the counterſcarp to a vaulted
gate, which croſſes the platform, the por-
ter of which keeps the peninſula every
evening under lock and key. One of the
redoubts, ſituated in the middle of the
lines, within cannon-ſhot each way, lined
with maſonry, and provided with artillery,
and ſome Turkiſh ſoldiers, together with
the commerce between the Ruſſians and
the Tartars, has given riſe to a miſerable
little village near this gate, where I alighted at the lodgings prepared for me. The
Governor of the Citadel loſt no time in
complimenting me on my arrival, by ſend-
ing me a trencher full of mutton, roaſted

in

in the Turkifh fafhion, which they call
Orman Kébab*. I foon after received a de-
putation alfo from the Janiffaries of the
fortrefs, inviting me to become a member
of their body, and I accepted their offer
with as much apparent readinefs, as they
manifefted to receive the prefent of my
welcome. The corps of Janiffaries, originally compofed of flaves carried off from
the Chriftians by the Turks, in time of
war, has been long recruited by their children, who are given as a tribute. But the
privileges granted to this new militia, determined the Turks to enroll their own
children amongft them. The abufes of
thefe privileges, and the number of candi-
dates, naturally going hand in hand, there
was no longer any fafety out of the pale of
their protection. The great men of the
empire enrolled themfelves ; the Grand
Signior himfelf wifhed to belong them,
and

---

* Orman Kébab,—the roaft of the woods.—This
is the favourite roaft meat of the Turks, and confifts
in pieces of mutton, cut and fpitted alternately with
flices of onions, roafted at a great fire.

and nobody difcovered that this was the
very method to increafe their infolence.—
The eftablifhed regulations for a long time
fupported this corps, in fpite of its irregularities, but they at length ceafed to maintain their independence.   Each Janiffary
became poffeffed of property; and connected at this day with the general order, by
the particular intereft of its members, this
corps is nolongerformidable to its mafters.

   Whilft I was taken up with thefe different affairs, I faw a troop of Europeans appear, efcorted by the Tartars of the plain.
They were Germans, fugitives from Ruffia, taken by the Noguais.   The fituation
of thefe unfortunate people, induced me to
claim them ; and they were immediately
delivered to me.   I refigned to them the
pyramid of roafted mutton, which they
certainly ftood more in need of than myfelf.   I then examined my new colony,
which was compofed of feven men, five
women, and four children.   They were
dejected by misfortune, but began to fmile
at the profpect of better days.   Thefe unhappy

happy people, born in the Palatinate, had
been drawn into Ruffia by the hopes of bet-
tering their fortune, (the motive of all emigrations) but the difappointment of which
makes them foon regret the lofs of their
former habitations. Imprifoned in a foreign country, their only projeƈt was to
make their efcape, and they knew no other
road but the wrong one. Arrived in the
defart plains, they had fcarcely time to
draw the breath of liberty, before the Noguais feized them, to fell them to the firft
purchafer. It afforded me great pleafure
to have faved thefe poor people, and I took
the neceffary meafures to infure their fafe
arrival at Baƈtchèferay.

I employed the reft of the day in examining the lines of Orcapi. No piƈture of
this kind can be more refpeƈtable. Excepting that the works are rather gigantic,
I know of none where nature is better feconded by art. The folidity of the en-
trenchment is likewife to be depended on.
It extends acrofs the ifthmus for three quarters of a league, and is flanked by two feas.
It

It overtops the plain below by about forty
feet ; and it will long continue to refift
that ignorance which neglects every thing.
Nothing points out the æra of its conftruction, but every thing confpires to prove it
of a date anterior to the Tartars ; or if not,
that thefe people were better informed in
antient times, at leaft, than they are at .
prefent.

It is very evident alfo, that if thefe lines
were pallifadoed *en fauffe braye*, as well
as the redoubts on them, and provided
with artillery, and above all, with how-
itzers, they would fecure the free poffeffion
of the Crimea againft an army of an hundred thoufand men.   Such an army, in
fact, unable to carry thefe lines by affault,
would be foon reduced to the neceffity of
retreating, from want of water.   It was
only by paffing a fmall marfhy arm of the
fea, to gain the head of a very narrow
tongue of land which opens parallel with
the eaftern fide of the Crimea, that the
Ruffians were able to penetrate into it in
the laft war.   This route had been already
fuccefsfully attempted in the campaigns
of

of 1736 and 1737, by General Munick ;
but this has neither fuggefted to the Tartars the defire nor the means of fecuring
themfelves in future from a fimilar misfortune, by defending the end of that tongue
of land, where the fmalleft refiftance would
be fufficient to check the progrefs of their
enemies.

On quitting Orcapi, I obferved that the
road was covered with a whitifh cruft, occafioned by the carriage of the falt which
the Tartars fell to the Ruffians. The falt-
works of Orcapi, part of the fovereign's
domain, are farmed out to fome Armenians and Jews ; and equally commercial,
and perpetual rivals, they augment the re-
venue, by bidding againft each other.—
They are fo unfkilful in the management
of their farms, and their avidity is fuch,
that they are always the dupes of their ignorance. They have no depofitory to receive, to dry, and to preferve the natural
falt which is formed in thefe falt-lakes ;
fo that the abundance of a plentiful feafon
cannot compenfate for the deficiency of a
bad one ; and the rains very frequently de-

E 5   ftroy

ſtroy this valuable production, which is ſo
eaſily preſerved in ſtore-houſes. The ſeller
and the buyer ſeem alſo to have combined
their ignorance in forming the conditions
by which they are reciprocally bound.
The buyer is allowed to come himſelf to gather the ſalt in the lakes, and to
load his carriages, which are to be drawn
by a certain number of horſes, and at a
ſtipulated price; but with this clauſe, that
if the carriage breaks down from its weight,
before it arrives at a given point, a penalty
and confiſcation follow. The buyer and
ſeller, in this contract, have overlooked the
certain loſs of what is ſcattered on the road,
and the diſadvantages reſulting from any
commerce founded on a perpetual ſtate of
warfare.

After paſſing the ſalt-works, we found
ourſelves in a country more remarkable for
its fertility than its cultivation; and a
number of villages, ſcattered over the
plain, afforded us a proſpect more intereſt-
ing, as it was long ſince we had enjoyed
ſo agreeable a ſcene. We arrived towards
the evening at a habitation, ſituated in the
bottom

bottom of a valley, where fome rocks announced to us a change of foil, and the
next day we got into a hilly country,
through which we travelled during the
whole morning. At noon we were obliged
to lock the four wheels of my carriage to
get it down a very narrow road, cut out of
the rock, which brought me to Baɛtchéfe-
ray. I arrived in this town early enough
to perceive all the inconveniencies to which
I fhould, thenceforward, be obliged to fubmit. Mr. Fornetty, Conful of France in
Tartary, received me in a houfe occupied
by him ten years, and which was defigned
for me. This houfe was not well calculated for the increafe of inhabitants I
brought with me; an inconvenience, above
all, very fenfibly felt by my attendants.
Fatigued as they were with a long journey, the fight of this ftrange land of promife completely difcouraged them ; and I
muft confefs, that my new dwelling could
not very well confole us for the nine hundred and thirty leagues we had travelled to
arrive there. An open wooden ftair cafe,

the

the fteps of which, rotted by the rain, giving way under the weight of every perfon
who mounted them, enabled the lighteft
amongft us to reach the only floor there
was ; which confifted of a hall, and two
fide rooms which ferved for falloon and
bed-chamber. The walls, formerly covered with lime and hair, as well as the
floor, difcovered to us the original conftruction of this building. It was doubtful whether my trunks would not prove
too heavy for it ; we tried the experiment,
however, with fuccefs, and as it is neceffary to make the beft of every thing, each
of us made choice of the fpot where we
were to reft from our fatigues.

If the fucceflive variety of objects on the
road prevents one from attending to any
thing but the difficulties to be furmounted
before the journey is at an end, that period naturally leads one to examine the nature of a fituation which is to be more per-
manent. This was our firft employment
on awaking. The time I had already paffed
with Mr. Conftillier, who accompanied
me

me as Secretary, made me very certain
that the fweetnefs of his difpofition, and
his patience, would get the better of every
inconvenience. I was as fortunate, likewife, in the choice M. de Vergennes had
made of Mr. Rufin to refide with me in
quality of Secretary Interpreter; and the
intimacy which very foon took place between thefe two young men, by giving
animation to their gaiety, rendered their
fociety more agreeable to me: It was, indeed, the only remaining fociety I had, for
I could not flatter myfelf with the profpect of deriving much advantage from a
Monk I had taken at Yaffi, and two Polifh
Armenian Miffionaries, any more than
from the company of Mr. Fornetty, who
was to leave me and return to Conftantinople as foon as his local and official information became unneceffary to me.

My arrival was immediately announced
to the Vifir of the Kam, and this Prime
Minifter, affuring me of the fatisfaction
his mafter would have in feeing me as foon
as I was difpofed to have my firft audience,
fent

fent me the eftablifhment of *Tayn*, affigned
me by the Prince. This cuftom confifts
in the fupplying with neceffary provifions,
the perfon whom it is meant to gratify.
Throughout the Eaft, gifts are always the
mark of honour; obliged, therefore, to
fubmit to this kind of diftinction, I tranf-
ferred my *Tayn* to the fubfiftence of my
little German colony; but although this
fuccour was fufficient to furnifh it abun-
dantly, my attendants faw no means of
providing for my perfonal wants. Reduced to bad bread, rice, and mutton, and
fome lean poultry, we were threatened, in
fact, with very indifferent living. I could
not conceive that I fhould want either butter, vegetables, or fifh, on the fineft foil
in the world, and in the neighbourhood of
the fea; but I foon underftood that celery
was cultivated as a rare plant in the Kam's
garden; that the Tartars did not know how
to make butter; and that the inhabitants
of the fea coaft were no better mariners
than thofe on the plains, therefore I was
obliged to fubmit. My fervants, however,

at

at length difcovered fome fpontaneous vegetables, which confoled us a little, and I
took meafures to get fome feeds from Conftantinople, aud hired a country houfe,
where I eftablifhed my Germans, to whom
I gave fome cows ; and my new farm very
foon fupplied me with abundance of every
thing. I determined, alfo, to make my
own bread : one of my fervants became an
excellent baker ; and the pleafure of having found out the means of obtaining it,
gave an additional relifh to our good
cheer.

I was waiting for fome prefents for the
Kam, which never arrived, before I had
my firft audience ; but the impatience of
Makfoud-Gueray, then on the throne of
the Tartars, removed every difficulty. On
the day appointed for the delivery of my
credential letters, the Mafter of the Ceremonies waited on me with a detachment
of the guard, and fome officers appointed
to efcort me to the Palace. Our cavalcade,
half European, half Tartar, drew together
a great concourfe of people. We alighted

in

in the laft court, and the Vifir, who was
waiting for me in the veftibule of the Palace, conducted me into the audience chamber, where we found the Kam feated on
the corner of a fopha. A chair was placed
oppofite to him, where I feated myfelf,
after paying my compliments to the Prince
and delivering my credentials. This firft
ceremony, which inftalled me in my public capacity in Tartary, was followed by
the civilities practifed amongft the Turks,
and by an invitation from the Kam to vifit
him frequently. I was then conducted
back to my own houfe in the fame order.
The following days were taken up in paying the neceffary minifterial vifits. I endeavoured alfo to form fuch connections as
might gratify my defire of becoming acquainted with the government, the manners, and the cuftoms of the Tartars; and
the Mufti, a man of abilities, of ftrict honour, and capable of a ftrong attachment,
was one of thofe with whom I formed the
greateft intimacy, and from whom I derived the moft ufeful information.

After

After attending principally to thefe objects, I thought it neceffary to endeavour, before the winter attacked me in my hut, to fecure myfelf againft the inclemency of the weather, and to enlarge and repair it, which was pretty nearly the fame thing as to rebuild it. We were now in the month of November, and no time was to be loft. I drew the plan, I collected the materials, and fuperintended the work, without departing from the method of building purfued by the Tartars; and I got tolerably well lodged before the end of December, at the expence of fix thoufand livres, (about 250l. fterling.) I fhall take this opportunity of defcribing the ftructure of the houfes in Crimea; but thefe details, or the architecture of the Tartars, will be of more fervice to the lovers of œconomy, than to difciples of Vitruvius.

Pillars placed on the points which terminate the angles, and the openings fixed perpendicularly by an architrave which fupports the joifts, prepares the way for the execution of the upper part of the building,

ing, which is formed in the fame manner
to receive the roof. The building thus difpofed, other pillars which are fmaller, at
a foot's diftance from each other, but per-
pendicular alfo, occupy the folds, and are
defigned to hold together the hazle ıods,
which give the houfe the appearance (f a
bafket; pounded earth, and cut ftraw, are
then applied to this fort of hurdle, after
which a layer of lime and hair, laid on in-
ternally and externally, added to the paint-
ing of the pillars, the doors, the plinths,
and the windows, give the whole of the
building a very pleafing appearance.

I muft add, that this manner of building has infinitely more folidity than might
be imagined from the defcription, and is
certainly more falutary than that of our
peafants houfes. I am farther convinced,
that gentlemen of eftates, who, either
from motives of intereft or benevolence,
are defirous of building houfes with the
view of increafing and favouring the population of their dependants, would gain in
every way by adopting this new plan of
building,

building, in which they would find great
œconomy, and enable the inhabitants to
make their own repairs, which will certainly appear the moſt important advantage.

Having now got a tolerable dwelling,
and in a very ſhort time, it became neceffary for me to look out for furniture. My
ſteward was the upholſterer, and I took
upon myſelf the joiner's work, and the
turnery; theſe occupations, together with
my private affairs, and my viſits to the
Kam, gave me a continual and varied employment, which filled up all my time.

Makſoud-Gueray had admitted me into
his private parties, which were compoſed
of Sultan Nouradin, his nephew, a Mirza
of the Chirins †, called Kaia-Mirza ‡, who
was the huſband of a Sultana, couſin-ger-
man to the Kam; of the Kadi-Leſker, and
of

† Chirin is the name of the moſt diſtinguiſhed family amongſt them, which compoſes the principal
Nobility of Tartary. We ſhall ſee, in the courſe of
theſe Memoirs, that the eſtabliſhed order excludes
from this claſs all the ennobled families.

‡ Kaia, in Tartar language, means Rock.

of fome other Mirzas. This Prince ufed
to receive us after the prayer of fun-fet,
and keep us 'till midnight. More diffident
from fyftem than from difpofition, Makfoud-Gueray, eafily prepoffeffed, recurred
with the fame readinefs to whatever could
reftore the tranquillity of his mind, and
render every thing agreeable about him.
With more knowledge than ufually falls
to the fhare of the Orientals, he was fond
of literature, and difcourfed on it with fatisfaction. Sultan Nouradin, brought up
in Circaffia, fpoke but little, and only
talked of the Circaffians. The Kadi-Lefker, on the contrary, was very loquacious, and talked of every thing ; ill informed, but of a lively difpofition, he very frequently departed from the gravity of his
fituation, to enliven our converfations.—
Kaia-Mirza furnifhed all the news of the
day ; whilft I entertained them with thofe
of Europe, and anfwered all their trouble-
fome queftions. The etiquette of this
Court allows very few perfons to be feated
in the prefence of the Sovereign; the Sultans

tans have this privilege by birth, except
the children of the Prince, who, from refpect, never fit down before their father.
This privilege is granted alfo to the heads
of the law, to the Minifters of the Divan,
and thofe of foreign Courts ; but excepting Kaia-Mirza, who was feated in quality
of hufband of a Sultana, the other courtiers ftood at the foot of the fopha, and
withdrew at fupper time. This repaft was
ferved on two round tables, one of which
fpread before the Kam, was fet apart for
his Tartar Majefty, who ufually eats alone,
and never departs from that etiquette but
in favour of fome Sultan diftinguifhed by
his age, or who is himfelf a Sovereign.
The fecond table, prepared in the fame
room, is for the perfons whom the Kam
admits to fupper. I eat at this table with
the Kadi-Lefker, and Kaia-Mirza. Makfoud Gueray always amufed himfelf with
encouraging the little differences of opinion which arofe daily between the Judge
and me, and in which this Magiftrate appeared lefs anxious about the accuracy of
his

his reafoning, than the amufement of his mafter. Our fituations were fo different, that it was impoffible to difpute his favour by the fame means ; but I did not neglect thofe which I thought might pleafe the Prince. I had remarked that he was fond of fire-works, and the ignorance of his ar-tificers was ill calculated to gratify his tafte. I got ready the implements, prepared the materials, and inftructed my attendants ; and when I thought myfelf capable of ful-filling my object, I afked permiffion of the Kam to exhibit a fire-work on his birth-day. Accuftomed as he had been to fee nothing but fmoaky gerbs, bad crackers, and fmall rockets, badly filled, and ill directed, the fuccefs of my exhibition was complete.

I had forefeen that the Kam, after politely thanking me for the faltpetre I had been burning, would politely complain of the fhortnefs of the entertainment ; and I had prepared, by way of anfwer, fome electrical experiments, which I offered to exhibit as a little chamber fire-work, to

fill

fill up the remainder of the evening. The firſt effects of this phenomenon excited ſuch aſtoniſhment, that I had ſome difficulty in deſtroying the opinion of magic I ſaw ariſing in their minds, and which was gradually increaſed by every freſh experiment. The Kam, however, had the air of comprehending me, and was himſelf deſirous of being electrified. I gave him the ſtroke very moderately, but I handled the courtiers in ſuch a manner as to obtain the Prince's approbation.

The whole town reſounded the next day with the prodigies I had performed; and I was obliged, on the following days, to ſatisfy the curioſity of thoſe who had not been preſent with the Kam at the firſt experiments. Several perſons ſucceſſively applied to me to repeat them upon them and their friends, and I ſent every body away equally full of amazement. Nothing was talked of but electricity, and the number of the curious continually increaſed.—I began, however, to be tired of the inconveniencies of this celebrity, and was

com-

complaining of it one evening to Mr. Ruffin, who was as tired of it as myfelf, when
we faw upwards of twenty lanthorns appearing in a row. I immediately fent Mr.
Ruffin to inquire of this troop the motive
of their vifit ; to whom their fpokefmen
addreffed the following difcourfe :—" We
are, Sir, Circaffian Mirzas, hoftages with
the Kam; we have heard of the miracles
performed by your Bey §, at his pleafure ;
miracles, of which no perfon before has
ever had an idea, fince the birth of the
Prophet, and which will never be known
to man after his death; befeech him to permit us to be witneffes to them, that we
may one day teftify them in our country;
and that Circaffia, deprived of this phœnomenon, may, at leaft, be able to record the
memory of it in her annals."

The gravity with which Mr. Ruffin delivered this harangue, preferved all its ri-
dicule.

§ Bey ;—the title given to perfons of diftinction,
and is equivalent to that of Signeur, or Lord, and is
ufed alfo for a Prince ; as Bey of Wallachia, Bey of
Moldavia.

dicule. I made my new guefts mount into
the faloon, where ranging them in a femi-
circle, with all the refpeft, and all the af-
feftation of myftic devotion, the Circaffian
orator addreffed the fame compliment to
me which he had done to my interpreter.
I liftened to his harangue with all the fo-
lemnity I was mafter of, and in my turn,
complimented all Circaffia ; after which,
I difpofed myfelf to imprefs ftrongly on
their minds the remembrance of eleftricity,
whilft Mr. Ruffin, offering them the ufual
civilities, amufed himfelf with heighten-
ing thofe ideas of the marvellous exploits
which had procured me their company.

It is eafy to imagine, that in this difpofition, I had no difficulty in felefting my
victims ; each fpeftator would be eleftrified in his turn ; and thefe poor creatures,
whom I fometimes pitied, gave a laugh of
fatisfaftion, in fuffering martyrdom, and
I was obliged to give my Circaffians fome
of the rudeft fhocks, before I had the good
fortune to difmifs them fully fatisfied ; but
they were the laft whom I eleftrified, and

VOL. II.   F   I endea-

I endeavoured to procure myfelf fome lefs
brilliant, but more ufeful amufement. My
uniform, which I always wore, threatened
to fall in pieces, and I tried to be my own
taylor. I had alfo the fancy to equip a
handfome Arabian horfe in the French
manner. I could not break him with a
Tartar faddle, the fhape of it raifing the
rider too far from the horfe. This was
no fmall undertaking, for I had to begin
with making the implements. I prepared
the faddle-bow, difpofed all the parts, and
at length completed a faddle of crimfon
velvet, with houfing, and trapping well
forted. I made ufe of it the firft time I
rode out with the Kam. This Prince had
the condefcenfion to admit me to be of all
his parties, and I was happy to give him
fome idea of our manner of riding.——
The Tartars know no other principle of
equitation than firmnefs in the feat, and
that firmnefs is carried even to roughnefs,
fo that the fupplenefs of the motions of
my Arabian horfe aftonifhed the whole
court. The Prince's firft Equerry was defirous

firous of trying him, but fcarce had he got aftride a bare faddle, before he was obliged to recover his equilibrium, by thrufting in his heels. My horfe, not accuftomed to the manœuvres of fuch a cavalier, would foon have got rid of him, had not his fervants run to his affiftance, and prevented the cataftrophe.

The Kam invited me alfo to his parties of hawking and greyhound courfing, which were very frequent. He was attended by five or fix hundred horfemen, and in this manner we ranged the neighbouring plains, where the abundance of game, joined to the vanity of the fportfmen, rendered thefe parties very lively. Makfoud-Gueray was particularly fond of hawking; his birds were perfectly well trained, and he wanted nothing but good dogs to ftart the game. I had brought one with me from France, of remarkable beauty, but he was fo careffed, fo fpoiled, fo wilful, that I never took him out with me, the very circumftance that made them think him of great value. The courtiers fpoke of him to the

Prince,

Prince, who expreſſed to me his deſire of
having him, and even reproached me with
a ſort of affeƈtation for having concealed
him. In vain did I aſſure him that my dog
was ill trained, that he would certainly
throw himſelf upon the birds, and that
ſome diſagreeable circumſtances would
happen ; he took all this for an excuſe, and
I was obliged to give way to his fancy,
which he very ſoon had reaſon to repent of.
I immediately ſent for my dog ; he arrived,
and began to pay his court very familiarly.
There was a baſon of water in the middle
of the apartment ; *Diamond* waſhes himſelf in it, jumps on the ſopha to careſs me,
and taking the laugh of the Kam for a
friendly invitation, leaps briſkly upon
him, overthrowing, as he paſſes, every
thing in his way. In the firſt moments of
favour, it is permitted to err with impunity ; *Diamond*, therefore, given into the
care of a page, from that evening he had
free quarters, and a grand hawking party
was ordered for the next day. Nothing
was talked of the whole evening but the
talents

talents of the new favourite; as for my
part, I fpoke of nothing but his vivacity
and frowardnefs; every thing about him,
however, was found charming, and the
Kam was fo impatient to fee *Diamond* in
action, that he gave us the rendezvous for
an earlier hour than ufual next morning.
On arrival, I perceived the hero of the en--
tertainment, led by his page, furrounded
by fpectators, and not knowing what they
were going to do with him; they were waiting for me, to give him his liberty. I had
hardly loofed him before the cavalry put
themfelves in motion, to open to the right
and left of the Kam, near whofe perfon I
was. *Diamond*, terrified at firft, was only
afraid of being crufhed. A quail, however,
rifes before him; one of the Kam's faul-
cons is flown at the game; he comes up
with and ftrikes his prey, and continues
his flight to fome diftance, where a faul-
coner, full fpeed, rides up to take him.
Diamond alfo fets off,—a double prey ani-
mated his ambition; and had not they
thrown a hammer at him, to make him
quit

quit his hold, my prediction would have been accomplifhed ; but the dog and the faulcon being both frightened, took different ways home, and the Kam was let off for the apprehenfion of lofing his bird.

My pofition with refpect to Makfoud-Gueray, and his Minifters, with the manner in which I had fucceeded in arranging my new eftablifhment, rendered my ftay at Baotchéferay, fupportable.   I was particularly intimate with Kaia Mirza, of the family of the Chirins, accounted the firft nobility of the Tartars : he had married a Princefs of the blood, who filled the place of Olou-Kanè, Governels of the Crimea ; and this Sultana, willing to give me a mark of her favour, fent me, by the intendant of her houfhold, a prefent of a night-fhirt, richly embroidered, and every thing belonging to the moft complete and magnificent defhabille.   The myftery with which this miffion was accompanied, might have given me fome uneafinefs ; in fact, the Princefs was feventy years old ; but I was foon made eafy on that head.   I was informed

formed that prefents of this kind are never made by a Sultana, but to one of her relations, and I gave way, without fear, to all my gratitude. The Princefs had fome intereft with Makfoud-Gueray, but her credit would probably have proved infufficient to preferve one of her favourites from the avarice of that Prince.

Yâcoub Aga, Governor and Grand Mafter of the cuftom-houfe of Balta, was on the point of falling a victim to it. Difpoffeffed of his employment, defpoiled of his fortune, and chained in prifon, he was in danger of lofing his head, notwithftanding the zeal of his protectrefs. It appeared to me very important to endeavour to fave, and re-eftablifh this man, with whom France had always great reafon to be contented. The Minifters feconded me ; the Mufti affifted us with ardour, as well as the Sultana ; Yacoub Aga quitted his chains to refume his ancient dignity, and the means of again laying the foundation of his fortune, which the Kam would not reftore him. But if this Prince may juftly be reproached

proached with this inftance of avidity, it
muft be owned that he vigoroufly fupported good order, without adopting the fana-
tical and fuperftitious principles which
lead the Turks to deviate fo often from it.
The flave of a Jew has murdered his mafter
in his vineyard; the complaint is made by
the neareft relations. The murderer is apprehended, and, previous to his trial, fome
zealous Mahometans prevail on him to become a Turk, in hopes of obtaining for
him a pardon. The converfion of the
criminal was oppofed to the fentence of
death pronounced by the Kam: it is proper
to obferve, that by the Tartar law the criminal muft perifh by the hand of the injured perfon, or by his heirs. It was object-
ed then, but in vain, that a Turk could not
be delivered up to the Jews. " I would deliver up my brother to them," replied the
Kam, " if he was guilty; I leave Provi-
dence to reward his converfion, if it be fin-
cere; it is my duty to do juftice." The
intrigues of the devoted Muffulmen fucceeded, however, in deferring the execution

tion until Friday afternoon, in order to
render that law favourable to the profe-
lyte, which obliges the injured party to
execute the fentence in four and twenty
hours, and the law compelling the Jews to
fhut themfelves up for their fabbath at fun
fet. The murderer, however, loaded with
chains, was conducted to the butt appropriated to this fort of execution; but a new
obftacle prefented itfelf. The Jews muft
not fhed blood; a public crier is fent
through the town to offer a confiderable
fum to any Jew who will lend his hand,
and it was amongft the moft wretched of all
people that this refearch was fruitlefs. This
new incident was reported to the tribunal
of the Kam, and the bigots expected to derive great advantage from it, but they were
deceived in their expectations. Makfoud-
Gueray permitted the Jews to execute the
criminal according to the law of the old
Teftament, and the fcene terminated by
ftoning him to death.

The Turkifh law, of which I have formerly fpoken, that which delivers over the

F 5   criminal

criminal into the hands of the injured
party, is founded on the Coran, which
grants to the neareft relation of the deceafed, the right of difpofing of the murderer's blood. We have feen that in Turkey, the party complaining *affifts* at the
punifhment; the Tartar law, more literal,
obliges them to carry it into execution. I
fhall further obferve, that amongft the
Turks, where the executioner does not give
the blow until the fum offered by the criminal be refufed, there are inftances where
the wife has fold the blood of her hufband.
In Tartary, on the contrary, the wife,
who is to plunge the knife with her own
hand into the criminal, never fuffers herfelf
to be tempted by any offer; and the law
which commits her vengeance to herfelf,
renders her inacceffible to every other fen-
timent.   One of the Prince's officers,
with his arm uplifted, carrying a filver
axe, precedes the criminal, conducts him
to the place of punifhment, and affifts at
the execution.

There

There is no country where crimes are less frequent than in Tartary. The plains, where malefactors might eafily efcape, afford very few objects of cupidity; and the peninfula of the Crimea, where there are more temptations, being daily fhut, leaves no hope of efcaping from punifhment. For this reafon no precautions are taken for the fecurity of the capital, in which there are no guards but thofe of the fovereign. The Palace he inhabits, formerly built entirely in the Chinefe, but repaired in the Turkifh fafhion, ftill retains fome of the beauties of its former ftile of conftruction. It is placed at one of the extremities of the town, and is furrounded by very high rocks, from whence flows an abundance of ftreams, which are conveyed into the kiofks and gardens in a moft delightful manner. This fituation, however, which looks on nothing but barren rocks, obliges the Kam very frequently to walk upon the heights, to enjoy the beauties of the moft variegated profpect.

I have

I have faid that the plains of the Noguais, which extend along the continent
of the Crimea, are nearly on a level with
the fea, and that the ifthmus forms another
level plain, thirty or forty feet higher.
This upper plain occupies the northern
half of the peninfula, and afterwards the
face of the country thick-fet with rocks,
and full of mountains running from weft
to caft, terminate in the pyramid of *Tcha-
dir-Dagu:*, the hill of the tent. This
mountain, which is too near the fea for its
bafe to add much to its elevation in the atmofphere, can only be claffed amongft the
mountains of the fecond order; but if we
caft an eye on the map of our hemifphere,
it is impoffible not to perceive that *Tchadir-
Dagu:* forms a part of that chain which
connects the Alps with Mount Caucafus.
In fact, we fee that the branch of the Ap-
penines which croffes Europe from weft to
caft, feparating Germany from Italy, Poland from Hungary, and Wallachia from
ancient Thrace, after plunging into the
Black Sea, re-appears in the fame direction,

on

on the fouthern part of the Crimea, fcarcely leaving a paffage for the communication
of the feas of Sabache, and the Pont-
Euxine, and continues as far as the Caf-
pian Sea, under the name of Caucafus,
once more to re-appear under that of Thibet, and to ftretch to the very eaftern extremities of Afia.

The continued feries of thefe mountains
too, is as evident, and as clearly demon-
ftrated by all the details we have refpecting their appearance, their ftructure, their
foffil productions, and the minerals they
contain.

The firft obfervation which prefents itfelf in the Crimea, is the uniformity of a
bed of rocks which crowns the top of all
the mountains on the fame level. Thefe
rocks, very fharp pointed, and of more or
lefs thicknefs, offer the moft indifputable
traces of the operation of the waters; one
diftinguifhes throughout them an exact refemblance to thofe which are at prefent expofed to the efforts of the fea, and are alfo
ftrewed with apparently foffil oyfters, but

fo

fo faftened, that they cannot be procured
without loofening them with a chifel. It
is obfervable, likewife, that the living
oyfter; of thefe foffils, which are of the
largeft kind, is not known in the feas of
the Levant.   I fhall add, that there are at
prefent no oyfters on the northern coaft of
the Black Sea, and that on the fouthern
part there is only the fmall kind.

Amongft the foffils adhering to the rocks
is found alfo the fea urchin, the living
animal of which is peculiar to the Red Sea.
The vallies which furrow that part of the
Crimea, contain very great beds of uni-
valve foffils, almoft all of the genus of
the Chinefe bonnet.   Thefe foffils differ,
however, from thofe we find in the Me-
diterranean, by a thicker fhell, lefs hollowed, and covered with circular ftripes ; in
fome valleys they are in fuch quantities,
as to choke all vegetation; thefe fhells are
there mixed with fragments of a foft fandy
ftone, imprinted with leaves, and branches,
the principal bed of which lies in the bottom of the ravines.

The

The level of the beds of rocks which I
have afcertained from one mountain to
the other, with the level of the fea, proves
that they are all equally horizontal. I
have always given the moft fcrupulous attention to my refearches into a fubject as
new, as it is interefting; and I have difcovered no exception to this uniformity *.
The map of the upper parts of the Crimea, taken from the level of thefe beds of
rock, would exhibit nothing but an archi-
pelago, a heap of iflands, more or lefs elevated, at a fmall diftance from each other,
and always to the weft of Caucafus, but
very diftant from the lands, which at that
epocha might form the continent towards
the

---

* When human knowledge fhall have penetrated
into the principles of the revolutions of the globe, the
obfervations I now report of the immutability of the
foil of the Crimea, will become more important : it
will prove that the caufes of the great convulfion have
had no effect on that peninfula. Earthquakes, which
are fcarcely known there, can never have been cen-
tral, the fummit of the rocks is ftill covered with
a vegetable earth, and the higheft mountains fhew
no marks of craters, nor the leaft veftiges of lava.

the north ; and it is only towards the Little
Don, that the earth begins to rife to the
fame level.

Such refearches into primitive geogra-
phy, by affifting the progrefs of human
knowledge, might throw a new light on a
fubject which has long been occupied by
the fpirit of fyftem. The philofophers
who are curious to know the original afpect
of the globe, may difcover it by following
the level of thofe features which are every
where the moft diftinctly marked. The
loftieft mountains will prefent to them le-
vels which had been firft abandoned by
the waters ; but, limited in thefe Memoirs
to the fimple narrative of the prefent appearance of the countries I have paffed
through, and of the character of their inhabitants, I fhall only add to what I have
faid on this fubject, the anfwer of a Tartar.
I was walking with this man in one of the
defiles, adjoining that in which Bactchéferay is fituated. I obferved there an iron
ring, placed on the top of an inacceffible
rock, which crowned and terminated the
bottom

bottom of this defile. I afked my Tartar
the ufe of this ring: " I imagine," replied he coolly, " that it ferved formerly to
faften veffels to, when the fea, bathing
thefe rocks, formed a harbour in this valley." I was confounded with this anfwer,
and could not help admiring the genius
which, with no other guide than the daily
comparifon of the banks of the fea, in their
prefent flate, with the antient traces of its
waters remaining on the mountains, could
elevate itfelf to the folution of the problem.
The ancient Greeks, and ancient Romans
too, had opportunities of admiring the moft
fublime *moral* philofophy of the Scythians;
but the vaft idea of the revolutions of our
globe is more aftonifhing, undoubtedly, in
a Tartar, and his unaffected fimplicity ftill
further increafed my admiration. We
may judge from him that his countrymen
intereft themfelves very little in the monuments which atteft the different ages of
nature. They neglect alfo to avail themfelves of her labours, by working the
mines of Tchadir-Dagué. The Genoefe,
better

better informed, and certainly more co-
vetous, had begun to extract the gold,
which is found in abundance in that mountain. It may alfo be prefumed that the
Kam would not have remained infenfible to
the acquifition of thefe riches, had not the
fear of exciting the avidity of the Porte led
him to prefer inactivity to a labour, of
which that government would have reaped
the benefit. Nor was the danger of feeing
thefe riches carried to Conftantinople, the
only one to which the Kam of the Tartars
would have been expofed, in working this
gold mine; by neceffarily introducing
perfons employed in the mint to direct
the works, he muft have introduced the
fcourge of prohibition into the Crimea,
and the Tartar fovereigns humanely facrifice their intereft in this particular, to
the public tranquillity. There is certainly
fome glory in being poor at this price.

Accuftomed to an exiftence, the pleafures
of which arife more from the richnefs of
the foil, than from that pride which im-
prifons itfelf under gilded roofs, the Tartars

tars make an article of luxury of the very air they breathe; and this firſt want of all beings is fully gratified by the beauty of the climate.

The meteors which one obſerves in the ſky of the Crimea, at all ſeaſons, and the whiteneſs of the *Aurora Borealis*, which are pretty frequent there, furniſh certain proofs of the purity of the atmoſphere. We may attribute this *ethereal* quality, if I may be allowed the expreſſion, to the immenſe dry plains to the northward of this country, and to the neighbourhood of Mount Caucaſus, whoſe ſummits attract, and abſorb all the vapours ariſing to the weſtward.

Regular ſeaſons, gradually ſucceeding each other, unite with the excellence of the ſoil, to favour the moſt luxuriant ve-getation. It conſiſts of a black virgin mould, mixed with ſand, the bed of which extends from Leopold in the Red Ruſſia, to this peninſula. The heat of the ſun brings to perfection all ſorts of grain with very little labour on the part of the culti-vator.

vator. This labour confifts, in fact, in fur-
rowing the land intended to be fown. Me-
lon feeds and aubergine ‡, peas and beans,
mixed together in a bag, are fcattered by a
man following the plough; they do not take
the pains to cover the feeds, but leave that
to be done by the rains, and the field is
quitted until the time of the different
crops, when they have nothing left to do
but to clear them from the confufion occafioned by this manner of fowing.

Amongft the number of fpontaneous
productions which cover the furface of the
Crimea, afparagus, walnuts, and filberts,
are remarkable from their fize. There is
likewife an aftonifhing quantity of flowers,
whole fields, covered with tulips of the
fmall fpecies, form, from the variety of
their colours, the moft pleafing picture.

The manner in which the vine is cultivated in the Crimea, is not calculated to
improve the quality of the grape. One
fees, with regret, that the moft beautiful

‡ Very common in France; refembling, if not the
fame as our egg plant, produced in hot houfes, &c.

expofures

expofures in the world cannot prevail on
the inhabitants to prefer thofe fituations to
the valleys; the vines are planted there in
holes of eight or ten feet diameter, by four
or five feet deep. The branches of the
vine are fupported on the edges of thefe
holes, covering the whole orifice with the
leaves, under which hang the grapes; deprived by this means of the fun, but abun-
dantly nourifhed by a foil always moift,
and fometimes drowned with the rain waters which collect there. They ftrip off
the leaves a month before the vintage, after
which they cut the vines clofe to the
ground; and the vineyard, under water
during the winter by the overflowing of
the rivulets, is covered with all forts of
aquatic birds.

The moft remarkable of the different
fpecies of thefe birds which abound in
the Crimea, is a fort of wild goofe, longer
legged than ours, with feathers of a lively
brick colour. The Tartars pretend that
the flefh of this animal is very dangerous;

I was

I was defirous, however, of tafting it, and found no bad effects from the experiment.

There is no country where there are more quails than in the Crimea; and thefe birds fpread over the whole country during the fummer, flock together at the approach of autumn, to crofs over to the fouthern fhore of the Black Sea, from whence they pafs into a warmer climate. The order of their emigration is invariable. Towards the end of Auguft, the quails which are collected together in the Crimea, make choice of one of thofe ferene days, when the northerly wind blowing at funfet, promifes a fine night; they collect on the beach, begin their flight together, at fix or feven in the evening, and complete their paffage of fifty leagues by day-break, where the nets fpread on the oppofite fhore, and the fportfmen lying in wait, enfnare the emigrants.

The vaft plenty of waters in the Crimea, do not form there any remarkable river, and the proximity of the fhore attracts every rivulet to the fea. The greateft heats

never

never dry up the fprings, and the inhabitants find in every hollow the moft delici-
ous water, which by running alternately
through agreeable meadows, and falling
amongft rocks, is beautifully limpid. The
Italian poplar is fond of growing near it;
and the quantity of thofc trees might make
them to be looked upon as natives of the
Crimea, did not the eftablifhments of the
Genoefe point out from whence they have
been tranfplanted.

That nation, which long governed by
its induftry, had extended its commerce
and its conquefts even into the Tauric
Cherfonefus, where the defcendants of the
famous Gengis-Kan were compelled to fubmit to the oppreffion of thefe merchants,
until the reign of Mahomet the Second,
who only freed the Tartars from the tyranny of the Genoefe, to fubftitute as heavy, perhaps, but certainly not fo humiliating a yoke.

The traveller ftill fees in the Crimea,
the remains of thofe chains which bound
the Tartars, and kept them in fubjection

to

to the Genoefe. Thefe monuments of
their tyranny, atteſt at once the fear and
uneafinefs of the tyrants. It is only on the
ſteepeſt rocks that we find the traces of
their ancient habitations. The rock itſelf,
which ſerves as a foundation for thefe
ſtrong caſtles, is hollowed all round, and
ſtill exhibits the plan of their dwellings.
Their ſtables are ſtill to be feen, and the
mangers cut out of the rock. The greateſt part of thefe hollow ways communicate
with each other, and fome of them with
the upper town, by ſubterraneous paſſages,
the avenues to which are ſtill open. I
found in the middle of a pretty large hall,
a ſquare bafon of ten feet diameter, by feven
feet deep, filled at this day with human
bones. I ſhall hazard no conjecture on
this circumſtance, but content myfelf with
relating what may ſtill be feen, fince thefe
ruins are only at two leagues diſtance from
Bactchéferay. Several of thefe retreats,
cut out of the rock, are to be feen in the
Crimea, and always on mountains difficult
of accefs ; it may be prefumed, that they
ſerved

ferved as an afylum for the flocks of the
Genoefe, which fed on the plains in the
day time, and were fhut up by them during the night.

The fteepeft places have been at all times
the afylum of liberty, or the haunt of tyrants; rocks are, in fact, the fituations
the moft capable of diffipating the fears
which affail alike the oppreffor and oppreffed.

It is probable that the town of Caffa,
which is ftill the centre of the commerce
of the Crimea, had the fame pre-eminence
in the time of the Genoefe; but on confidering the beauty of the Port of Baluk-
lava, and fome ruins of ancient buildings,
one is led to imagine that they had not neglected to make ufe of it. This harbour
is fituated on the moft foutherly part of
the Crimea; the two promontories which
form the entrance, are the firft land which
appears to the north-eaft of the Thracian
Bofphorus. This port, befides its proximity, extent, and fecurity, is in the neighbourhood of forefts, which might furnifh

VOL. II.   G   fhip

fhip timber. At prefent totally abandoned, the port of *Baluk-lava* preferves nothing but the traces of its ancient importance, as we have already feen, that the
tombs ftill vifible at Krim, the ancient capital of the peninfula, are the only marks
of a town which was formerly of fome
confideration.

There are few towns in the Crimea
worthy of being mentioned. *Guez-levé*
merits however to be fpoken of, on account of its harbour, on the weftern fide
of the peninfula, and *Acmedchid*, the refidence of the Calga Sultan †.

After running over the principal objects
connected with the natural hiftory of the
Crimea, let us caft a more attentive eye on
the political fituation of the Tartars, and
on the principles of their government.

The countries comprized under the
name of Little Tartary, are the peninfula
of Crimea, the Cuban, a part of Circaffia,
and all that territory which feparates the
Ruffian empire from the Black Sea. This

† We fhall fee further what this dignity is.

zone,

zone, from Moldavia to near Taganrog,
fituated between the 46th and 44th de-
grees of latitude, is 30 or 40 leagues broad,
by near 200 long.   It contains from Eaft
to weft, the Yetitche Koulé, the Dgamboylouk, the Yedeffan, and Bafs-Arabia.
The latter province, called at prefent the
Boudjak, is inhabited by Tartars fettled in
villages, as well as thofe of the peninfula,
but the inhabitants of the three other provinces have only tents made of felt,
which they remove at pleafure.

Thefe people called Noguais, and who
are fuppofed to be wandering tribes, are
fettled however in the vallies which interfect the plains they inhabit from North to
South ; and their tents ranged along
them in one line, form a kind of villages
from 30 to 35 leagues in length, which
diftinguifh the different hords.

It is natural to imagine that the rural
and frugal way of life of this paftoral people, is more favourable to population than
amongft polifhed nations, where multiplied wants, and excefs of luxury, radi-

cally

cally deftroy it. It is obferved, in fact, that the population is already lefs confiderable, even under the roofs of the Crimea, and the Boudjak, than under the tents of the Noguais; but there is no other method of computing the number of the people than by the appearance of the military force the Kam is able to bring into the field. We fhall fee this Prince very foon levy three armies at the fame time; that which he commands in perfon of 100,000 men, that of his Calga of 60,000, and that of his Nouradin of 40,000. He might have raifed double the number, without prejudice to the neceffary labour; and if we confider the number of foldiers, and the furface of the Tartarian ftates, we may form fome comparifon between their population and ours.

The moft certain method of eftimating the power of thefe nations, is by feeing them act in armies. But it is well to begin by attending to the nature of their forces, and the means of collecting them.— Thefe means are connected with the government, and the origin of all government, forms an effential part of hiftory.

That of the Tartars, in particular, prefents the image of a vaft ocean, with the extent of which we never can become acquainted, but by following the courfe of the furrounding coafts. The annals of this people are to be found no where but amongft fuch nations as have had the misfortune to be near them, and which they have fucceffively over-run. Thefe very nations, however, who have written very little, or not at all, on the fubject, leave fcarcely any materials for hiftory beyond conjecture; but fuch as they are, on comparing them with the annals of all people, we are compelled to admit, that the Tartars, above other nations, have the beft afcertained claims to antiquity.

Without pretending to a profound inquiry into the great queftion which occupies the men of letters at this day, that of the true fituation of the ifland of the Atlantes, I fhall only obferve, on the platform of Tartary, which prolongs to
the

the north the chain of mountains of Caucafus and Thibet. As for the Ifle of Corea, judging from the courfe of the waters, which from the centre of Afia empty themfelves to the fouthward and northward of that part of the globe, it forms the moft elevated portion of thofe lands which feparate the feas of India from Kamftchatka. This obfervation a-lone feems to render it certain, that this country, poffeffed at prefent by the Tar-tars, muft have been the firft difcovered land in Afia, and the earlieft inhabited ; the fource of that population which firft fent forth thofe fwarms which, conftantly driven back by the wall of China, **and** the defiles of Thibet and of Caucafus, fell upon the northern parts of Afia, and overflowed our Europe, under the name of Goths, Oftrogoths, and Vifigoths.

Befides thefe geographical obfervations, this hypothefis is ftill further fupported by the Tartar tradition, communicated to me by Krim-Gueray. We fhall foon fee this Prince on the throne, and have rea-

fon

fen to admire his courage, his information, his philofophy, and death.

It would be difficult to extract any thing
fure and well afcertained, from the annals
of the Tartars, prior to Jengis-Kam ; but
we know that this Prince, elected Grand
Kam, by the Kams of the different tribes,
was only chofen to be the King of Kings,
becaufe he was the moft powerful amongft
them.   We know, likewife, that at this
period Jengis-Kam conceived and carried
into execution the projects of invafion on
which he founded the greateft empire recorded in hiftory. The emigrations fubfe-
quent to this conqueror, and which have
covered the conquered countries, prove alfo
the degree of population neceffary to fupply
thefe overflowings ; and all thefe circumftances combined, carry back the origin of
this family to the remoteft periods of time.

An uninterrupted fucceffion has continued to our days ; this dynafty of Princes
of the Jengis-Kam race, as well as the feudal government, which ftill prevails in
Tartary, amongft them, are ftill to be
found the firft laws by which *we* were governed—

verned—the fame prejudices which prevailed amongft us ; and if we combine
thefe refemblances with the emigrators of
this ancient people towards the north, and
thofe of the north towards us, we fhall
have no difficulty, perhaps, in acknow-
ledging the fource of our moft ancient
cuftoms.

After the Sovereign family, the next in
rank are the families of Chirin, of Man-
four, of Sedjoud, of Argifin, and of Ba-
roun. The family of Jengis-Kam furnifh
the Lords Paramount, and the five others
the five great vaffals of the empire.
Thofe who are called Beys, are always
reprefented by the eldeft of each family ;
and this is invariable. Thefe ancient Mirzas, whofe ftock is placed by the Tartar
annals amongft the companions of Jengis-
Kam, form, in the above gradation, the
great nobility of the country : they can
never be confounded with the ennobled
families. The latter, united under the de-
nomination of a Mirza *Capikouly*, that is
to fay, Mirza, flave of the Prince, have
neverthelefs, a Bey who reprefents
them,

them, and the rights of the great vaſ-
ſalage, that of ſitting in the aſſembly of
the ſtates. Amongſt the Mirzas *Capikouly*, the family of Koudalak, diſtinguiſhed by the ancient date of its creati-
on, enjoys the excluſive right of furniſhing from the eldeſt of its members, the
repreſentatives of all the ennobled families;
and theſe ſix Beys, joined to the Lord Paramount, form the Senate, the Select
Court, the Supreme power of the Tartars.

Theſe aſſemblies are never convoked but
on extraordinary occaſions, to prevent the
Kam, who has the privilege of calling together the grand vaſſals, from taking advantage of their abſence, to extend his authority beyond the bounds of the feudal
ſyſtem : the Bey of the Chirins conſtantly
repreſents the other Beys ; and this Chief
of the Tartar nobility, as well as the Sovereign, has his Calga, his Nouradin, his
Miniſters, and the right of calling together
the aſſembly of the Beys, ſhould this con-
vocation, neglected by the Kam, become
neceſſary to counteract even his deſigns.

G 5   The

The poft of Calga of the Chirins, is always held by the eldeft of the family, after the Bey; this chief, therefore, has
always his fucceffor near him, and this
counterpoife of the Sovereign's power is
always in action.

The fame conftitution which combines
all its forces againft the attempts of defpotifm, is equally jealous of the fecurity
and ftability of the lawful power of the
Sovereign. The great Tartar vaffals appear, in fact, to have no other connection
with the government, than as columns to
the edifice which they fupport, without
being able to fhake it. There is no example amongft this people of fuch trouble as
agitated France, during the whole period
of the exiftence of the feudal fyftem. The
Tartar government, ftill in its purity,
leaves no opening for ambition. In France
men were born great vaffals, in Tartary
they have hardly time to be fo.

It is probable that the fame order was
formerly eftablifhed in the Sovereign's family, and that the Kam of the Tartars was
always

always the eldeft member of that family;
but whatever was the order of fucceffion
before the arrival of the Genoefe in the
Crimea, at that æra, we plainly difcover
tyranny countenancing intrigues; three
Kams elected at a time, and Mingli-Gueray, who had the beft founded pretenfions,
was kept a prifoner at Mancoup.

Mahomet the Second had juft completed the conqueft of Conftantinople, and ex-
pelled the Genoefe: he then flew to drive
them likewife from the Crimea, and to
refcue Mingli-Gueray from their hands;
but he did not re-eftablifh him on the
throne, before he concluded a treaty with
that Prince, which gave to the Porte his
nomination, and that of his fucceffors. A
great part of Romelia was given as a de-
pendency to the Jengis-Kam Princes, rich
fucceffions were accepted as a price for the
liberty of the Tartar Sultans, and the gua-
ranty of their fubmiffion; and each Prince
of the reigning family, from that inftant,
formed hopes of attaining the throne by
his intrigues at Conftantinople.

Notwith-

Notwithſtanding the precaution of Mahomet the Second, conqueror of the Genoeſe in Tartary, to inſure the execution of his treaty with Mingli-Gueray, it is certain that the contracted parties could not really ſtipulate any thing, but in virtue of their reſpective rights; that thoſe of the Tartar Republic could not be compromiſed, and that the depoſing of the Lord Paramount of the Tartars, aſcribed to the Grand Signior, could convey no legal prejudice to the independence of the nation. The *jus publicum*, therefore, the public right of the Tartars, has been overlooked, or miſtaken by other powers, when they have taken upon them to pronounce *the independence of this nation.* To declare a nation free, which has never ceaſed to be ſo, is the firſt act of its ſubjection.

The political methods adopted in the Crimea to maintain a perfect equilibrium between the great vaſſals and the Paramount, rendered it neceſſary that the diſtribution of lands ſhould be ſuch as to enſure

fure its duration. But this partition itfelf
muſt partake of the different modes of
living of the inhabitants.

The lands of the Crimea, and of Baſs-
Arabia, are divided into noble fields, royal
domains, and lands held by foccage. The
firſt, which are all hereditary, do not hold
even of the crown, and pay no quit rent.
Thoſe of the domain are partly annexed to
certain offices by way of falary; the fur-
plus is diſtributed by the Sovereign to
whom he thinks proper. The *droit d'aubaine*, or *efcheat*, eſtabliſhed in the Crimea
in default of heirs in the feventh degree,
gives the Kam that privilege over every
thing which refpeċts the property of the
nobles; and each Minga poſſeſſes the fame
right over the property of the inferior
claſſes, in the whole extent of his fief. It
is on this principle, alſo, that the annual
poll tax is collećted from all the Chriſtian
and Jew vaſſals, and this latter objećt gives
the utmoſt extent of the moſt abſolute
property to the eſtates of the nobility of
Tartary.

It

It is only on the affembling of the ftates, likewife, that the Mirzas, poffeffors of fiefs, are bound to military fervice; but I fhall treat of this article when I come to the circumftances which bring all thefe details into action.

Thefe diftinctions of territorial property are not known amongft the Noguais; and this paftoral people, occupied entirely with their flocks, are left in the full enjoyment of their plains, knowing no other boundaries than thofe traced out between the neighbouring hords.

But if the Noguais Mirzas partake with their vaffals of the community of the foil, if they even affix a fort of difgrace to agriculture, they are not on that account lefs powerful. Retired during the winter in the vallies, occupied by the hords, each of them collects in his aoul †, the tribute which is due to him, in cattle and provifion; and when the fowing feafon comes, he goes into the plain with his hufband-

men,

---

† Aoul; part of a hord, which comprehends the vaffals holding under the fame noble.

men, fixes on the fpot for cultivation, and divides it amongft the vaffals.

By thus changing their tillage, the No-guais unite excellent pafturage with the moft plentiful crops, from lands which are never exhaufted.

The right of *Corveé*, or binddags, which having lefs connection, doubtlefs, with the feudal fyftem, than with the luxury of the great vaffals and Lords of fiefs, prevails likewife in the Crimea, is unknown to the Noguais ; but they pay a tenth to the Go-vernor of the province.

The Sultans, who are generally invefted with thefe governments, refide there un-der the title of *Scrafkers*, and command as Viceroys. But the firft dignity of the empire is *Calga*, always conferred by the Kam on one of the Princes of his houfe, in whom he places the moft confidence. His refidence is at Ackméchid, a town fituated at four leagues from Baëtchéferay, where he enjoys all the decorum of the fo-vereignty. His Minifters carry his orders into execution, and his jurifdiction ex-tends very near to Cafa.

The

The dignity of Calga, formerly deſtined for the preſumptive heir, ſtill preſerves the privilege of holding the reigns of government in caſe of the Sultan's death, and until the arrival of his ſucceſſor. He commands in chief the Tartar armies, when the Kam does not himſelf take the field; and he inherits, as Lord Paramount, the property of all the Mirzas who die within his dependencies, without heirs of the ſeventh degree of affinity.

The poſt of *Novradin*, the ſecond dignity of the kingdom, is held alſo by a Sultan, who has likewiſe the right of having Miniſters; but theſe, as well as their maſter, are without any active functions. This little Court, which has no other reſidence than Baſtchéſeray, is confounded with that of the Kam; ſhould ſome event, however, occaſion troops to be ſent into the field, the command of which is entruſted to the Novradin, his authority, as well as that of his Miniſters, acquires from that moment all the activity of the ſovereign power.

The

The third dignity of the kingdom, held by a Sultan under the title of Or-Bey, Prince of Orcapi, has fometimes been conferred on *Chirin-Mirzas*, who had efpoufed Princeffes of the blood royal. Thefe nobles, who difdain the firft places in the Miniftry, and will only accept of thofe deftined for the Sultans, have been allowed alfo to hold exterior governments; but thefe governments of the frontiers are generally poffeffed by the fons or nephews of the reigning Prince. They are Generals of the troops of their particular provinces; and when thofe of Boud-jak, Yedefan, and the Cuban, are called out, they are always commanded by the Sultan Serafkers, even after a junction with the forces under the Kam, the Calga, or the Nouradin.

The hord of the Dgamboylouk is governed only by a *Cuiamakan*, or Lieutenant of the King; he performs, therefore, the functions of Serafker, and conducts the troops to the army, and then refigns his command to the commander in chief, to return to his government, and to have an eye

to

to the fecurity of the plains, which are
fituated before the ifthmus of the Crimea.

Befides thefe principal employments,
the revenues of which arife from certain
duties collected in the provinces, there are
two *female* dignities. That of *Ala-Bey*,
which the Sultan commonly beftows on
his mother or one of his wives; and that
of *Ouloukany*, conferred on the eldeft of his
fifters or daughters. Several villages are
under the dependencies of thefe Princeffes, who take cognizance of the differences
between their fubjects, and diftribute juftice through their intendants, who fit for
that purpofe at the gate of the Seraglio,
the neareft to the harem.

I fhall enter into no details concerning
the Mufti, the Vifir, and the other Minifters, whofe offices are analagous to their
correfponding fituations in Turkey, with
this difference, that the principles and
cuftoms of the feudal government moderate their exercife in this country.

The revenues of the Kam fcarcely a-
mount to 600,000 livres, (about 31,000l.
fterling)

fterling) for the fupport of his houfhold;
but if this moderate income reftricts the
liberality of the Prince, it does not prevent him from being generous. A number of Mirzas live entirely at his expence,
until the *droit d'aubaine*, or efcheat I have
fpoken of, furnifhes him the means of
getting rid of them, by granting them
fome part of his domain.

Befides, the raifing of his troops puts
him to no expence. All the lands are
held by military fervice, nor does the Sovereign fupport any expences of juftice,
which is gratuitoufly diftributed throughout the whole of his extent of government,
as well as by the particular jurifdictions in
their refpective diftricts; appeals lie from
thefe fubordinate judicatures to the tribunal of the Paramount.

The moft complete education in Tartary, extends no farther than to the knowledge of reading and writing; but if the
inftruction of the Mingas be neglected,
they are diftinguifhed by an eafy politenefs
refulting from the habit of familiarity, in
which

which they accuſtomed to live with their
Princes, which never deviate into dif-
reſpeƈt.

Baƈtchéſeray, neverthelefs, contains a
very valuable hiſtorical journal, under-
taken by the anceſtors of a family who have
always preſerved, and carefully continued
it : This manuſcript, begun by its author,
by colleƈting the moſt ancient traditions,
contains all the fucceſſive faƈts down to the
prefent day. The event of my miſſion
into Tartary, occaſioned the perfon who
was continuing the journal, to apply to me
for fome information by which means I
diſcovered it. I made a fruitlefs attempt
to obtain fuch an acquiſition ; ten thoufand crowns (£ 1250 ſterling) could not
tempt him, and circumſtances did not allow me time to procure extraƈts from it.

The gazettes have faid enough of the
troubles which in our time have diſtraƈted
Poland, and of the difcuſſions between the
Porte and Ruſſia. Makfoud-Guéray found
himfelf in the very centre of this conflagration, and compelled to play a confiderable

rable part in it; he trembled for the confequences to himfelf, faw his fucceffor in
Krim-Gueray, and was not deceived in
any of his conjectures.

The affair of Balta, however, determined the Grand Signior to difplay the
ftandard of Mahomet. The Ruffian Minifter was fent to the Seven Towers; and
Krim-Gueray, replaced on the throne of
the Tartars, was called to Conftantinople,
to concert with his Highnefs the firft military operations. This news reached
Bactchéferay with the intelligence of the
depofing of Makfoud. The fame meffenger brought orders for the new Kam to
inftal a *Caïmakon* †, and for fixing the general rendezvous at Kaouchan, in Bafs-
Arabia. I haftened to go there, and was
preparing to meet Krim-Gueray at the
Danube, when I received a meffenger from
him, difpenfing with that formality, limi-
ting the ceremonial to my accompanying
him on his entry, affuring me of his favour,

† This title, which fignifies " holding place," anfwers to that of Regent.

and

and defiring me to prepare a fupper for him on the day of his arrival.

This opening appeared to me very flattering; but the fupper would have embarraffed me, had not the courier who conveyed the meffage given me the neceffary hints.   He was his confidential man.—— " Our mafter loves fifh," fays he, " he knows that your cook dreffes it very well; his own puts nothing but water in the fauces."   This was enough for me to difcover the Prince's tafte, and I gave orders for the beft fifh of the Neifter to be drowned in excellent wine.

The Kam was to make his entry the next day.   I mounted my horfe, and met him at two leagues diftance from the town. He was attended by a numerous cavalcade, and the reception he gave me, correfponded with the teftimonial of his favour which preceded him.

Krim-Gueray, about fixty years of age, joined to an advantageous fize, a noble carriage, eafy manners, a majeftic countenance, a lively look, and the happy talent
of

of affuming at pleafure the appearance of
gentle affability, or of a commanding feverity. The circumftance of the war
brought in his train a great number of
Sultans, feveral of whom were his children. His fecond fon was particularly
pointed out to me as a young man whofe
youthful courage was burning to diftinguifh itfelf, and who, from the habitual
exercife of his ftrength, was eafily able to
bend two bows at a time. He had purfued this exercife from his infancy; and
when this Prince was hardly nine years old,
his father, wifhing to pique his vanity, faid
to him, with a contemptuous air, that "a
diftaff fuited better a poltroon like him."
"Poltroon!" replied the child, turning
pale, "I fear nobody,—not even you!"
letting fly an arrow, which fortunately
ftruck only a bafket of wooden ware, into
which the iron tip of the arrow went two
fingers deep. As the greateft mildnefs,
as well as the general conduct of the child,
previous to this fit of paffion, gave proofs
of the ftrongeft filial refpect, fuch violence

can

can only be attributed, in this inftance, to an exceffive fenfibility on the point of honour.

Every thing neceffary was prepared at the gate of the town for the public entry and inftallation of the Kam, where he difmounted for a moment, to put himfelf in order, under a tent made ready for the purpofe. Dreffed in a cap loaded with two aigrets, enriched with diamonds, his bow and quiver flung acrofs his body, preceded by his guard, and feveral led horfes, whofe head-ftalls were ornamented with tufts of feathers, followed by the ftandard of the Prophet, and accompanied by all his court, this Prince repaired to his palace, where he received in the hall of the Divan, feated on his throne, the homage of all the grandees.

This ceremony employed us till the hour of the fupper I had prepared for him, and which my cook was permitted to ferve up. The Prince's cooks, apprized of this rivality, endeavoured alfo to diftinguifh themfelves, but they could not contend

againft

againſt the wine ſauces. They ſucceeded
no better in their made diſhes; and the
ſuperiority of the French kitchen procured
me the advantage of daily furniſhing a dozen of articles at all the Prince's entertain-
ments.

Krim-Gueray did not confine his taſte
to good cheer, every pleaſure had its
charms for him. A numerous orcheſtra,
a troop of comedians and buffoons, whom ⟨
he had alſo in his pay, by varying his
amuſements, filled up all his evenings, and
relieved him from the fatigues of political
affairs, and preparations for war, with
which the day was taken up.

The activity of this Prince, for whom
nothing was too arducus, made him require alſo a great ſhare of it from others,
and I may venture to ſay that I had the
good fortune to ſatisfy him. I had the
honour of his confidence, was admitted to
his parties of pleaſure, and I amuſed myſelf greatly with the curious and varied
picture of his court.

VOL. II. H Kaouch-

Kaouchan was become the centre of Tartary; all orders were iſſued from thence; people flocked there from all parts; and the croud of his courtiers augmented every day. The new Miniſters, whom I had known in the Crimea, and who perceived the particular favour with which I was honoured by the Kam, made choice of me to obtain from their maſter a favour they would not themſelves have preſumed to folicit. The experience of his former reign, had made them feel that it was of the laſt importance to keep him from a firſt act of ſeverity, which once committed, however repugnant at firſt to his diſpoſition, no perſon could tell where his cruelty would ſtop. An unhappy Tartar having acted contrary to too ſevere an ordinance, was condemned by the Kam to ſuffer death; preparations were making for conducting the wretch to the place of puniſhment, at the moment of my arrival at the palace; ſeveral Sultans immediately got round me, explained the circumſtance, and deſired me to preſerve the Tartars from

from the confequences of this execution.
I entered into the apartment of Krim-
Gueray, whom I found ftill agitated with
the efforts it had coft him to order the execution. I approached him, and incli-
ning myfelf to kifs his hand, which I had
never before done, I held it, notwithftanding the attempt he made to withdraw it.
" What would you have?" faid he, with
a look of feverity.—" The pardon of the
criminal," anfwered I. " What concern
can you have," replied he, "in this wretch's
fate?"--"None," added I; "a man who has
difobeyed you can infpire me with none;
it is only for you, Sire, that I am concern-
ed; you would foon become cruel, were
you, but for a moment, too fevere; and you
have no reafon to ceafe being good, to be
conftantly feared and refpected." He fmiled, and abandoning me his hand, I kiffed
it; and flew, by his defire, to announce
the pardon he had granted. The joy
produced by this circumftance was continued by a new Turkifh Comedy, of a tolerably burlefque kind. Krim-Gueray,
during the reprefentation, afked me many
queftions

queſtions about Moliere's plays, which he had heard ſpoken of. What I told him of the dramatic laws, and of the decency obſerved on our theatres, gave him a diſguſt for the farces with which the Turks are ſtill obliged to be ſatisfied. He perceived of himſelf, that the *Tartuffe* was preferable to *Pourceaugnac*; but he could not perceive how ſuch a character as the *Bourgeois Gentilhomme* could exiſt in a ſociety where the difference of rank is ſo perfectly underſtood, and ſo invariably eſtabliſhed; and I rather choſe to let him remain in ignorance, and imagine the poet was in the wrong, than to undertake his juſtification, by expoſing the hiſtory of our irregularities. " But," added he, " if it be impoſſible to carry on the deception refpecting *birth*, a man may eaſily impoſe upon the world by his character. Every country has its *Tartuffes*; (hypocrites) Tartary has hers;— and you will oblige me by getting this piece tranſlated *.

Whilſt

* Mr. Rufin, Secretary Interpreter of the King at Verſailles, undertook this work. His underſtanding would

Whilft our imagination was occupied by
thefe peaceful projeɔts, an Envoy from the
Confederates of Poland arrived at Kaouchan, to concert with the Kam the opening of the campaign. This Prince had
promifed the Grand Signior to begin by an
incurfion into New Servia: the Polifh
Ukraine might fuffer by this, and it required, therefore, fome preliminary ne-
gociations, to which the powers of the
Polifh Envoy appeared infufficient. Time
preffed, however; and Krim-Gueray was
defirous that I fhould go to the neighbourhood of Kotchim, to treat, in his name,
with the principal Confederates, who had
taken refuge there. But, flattered as I
was with this mark of the Prince's confidence, I did not choofe to accept the com-
mifiion without a Tartar colleague, who
was named on the fpot, and, as well as
myfelf, was invefted with full powers.
Our Embaffy required more difpatch than
luxury, and we flept the very next day
within

would have laid the foundation of good tafte amongft
the Tartars, had circumftances permitted him to de-
dicate his time to it.

within the confines of Moldavia. The
picture of the moft horrid devaftation preceded even the war in that country; and
the terror of the inhabitants from the incurfions alone of fome troops had already
occafioned this calamity. The defertion
of the villages, and the ceffation of all huf-
bandry, did not promife that abundance of
provifions for the fubfiftence of the Ottoman army, which they had reafon to ex-
pect on the borders of the Danube; but
thefe reflections, which I made to my colleague, feemed to intereft him infinitely
lefs than the fcarcity we were then fuffering, until our arrival at Dankowtga †.
The Counts Crazinfki and Potocki, received us there with all the refpect due to
the Prince we reprefented; but the excellent Tokay wine with which they regaled
us, gave much more pleafure to the Tartar Ambaffador. I had brought him in
my carriage; but the inconvenience of an
elevated feat, made him defire a Turkifh
waggon

† A village near Kotchim, whither the Confederates retired after the declaration of war.

waggon for his return, in which he might
lie at his eafe.   I made a point of procuring this fatisfaction for a man whofe great
age, and amiable character, were equally
interefting.   A waggon followed with our
baggage and fome fervants.   We travelled
in this manner by a different road, which
we were affured was better, although fome-
what longer.   Very heavy falls of fnow,
were juft fucceeded by a pretty fevere froft;
it was neceffary to avail ourfelves of this
circumftance to pafs at Gac-le Pruth, before the fwell of the river, which would
be occafioned by the flighteft thaw.   Conducted by a guide, we reached the borders
of that river, where the ice was drifting
rapidly with the current.   I was unacquainted with the depth of it, and was
afraid of the experiment; but my conductor encouraged me, by going before my
carriage, which led the way.   It was
drawn by fix good horfes, and was heavy
enough to refift the current, and confequently arrived fafe on the oppofite fide.   I
haftened to get on fhore to look after the

two

two waggons, for which I was uneafy on
account of their lightnefs. They were
fcarcely a third of the paffage before the
water began to lift them up. I called to
them to flop; but inftead of liftening to
me, the poftillions bear up their horfes,
the two carriages are overfet, and in an
inftant the river hurries them along pell
mell, with the flakes of floating ice. I fly
to the poftillion of my carriage, to order
him to unharnefs his horfes, and go to the
affiftance of the Tartar Envoy and my
people ; I find him on the bank expiring
with cold ; I drag him near an adjoining
ditch, where I precipitate him, and cover
him with fnow. My coachman had already followed the courfe of the river as
far as a mill, where, by his cries, he had
drawn the attention of the millers. I arrive there foon after, and find them employed in fifhing up, with crooks, thofe
who had been under water. But I fearch
in vain for my ancient colleague, and I was
agitated with the utmoft violence of de-
fpair for his fate, when I heard his voice,
defiring

defiring me to calm myfelf, whilft he was in the midft of the flakes of ice, and his head barely out of water, peeping through the door of his carriage. He was only ftopped by a fhallow place, from whence the fmalleft force would have detached him. I was at length fortunate enough to relieve him, and to collect together all my fhipwrecked companions, whom it was ftill neceffary to preferve from the danger of perifhing with cold; and, in fact, the froft had fo hardened their cloaths, that they could not be ftripped until the heat of a good fire had foftened the ftuff. As foon as I was fure that the care of the millers would be fufficient for them, I ran with my coachman to bring back my poftillion, who was recovered by the fnow. We faw him, on our arrival, employed in getting out of the hole, into which I had thrown him : the good fire at the mill completely reftored him; and I was agreeably fur-prized, on my return, to find all my bag-gage fifhed up. I provided in the beft manner I could for the frefh fuccours

H 5   which

which the circumftances required, and I
foon had time to fympathize with my colleague, who having himfelf run the greateft rifque, would fpeak of nothing but my
anxiety on his account. The time neceffary for drying their cloaths, putting our
waggons in order, and victualling our
troop, delayed our departure until the next
day. Hitherto I had no reafon to praife
the route we had taken ; and the bad roads
we met with would have compleatly dif-
gufted me, had it not been for the hope
of very foon arriving at Botouchan. This
was defcribed to me as one of the moft confiderable towns in Moldavia—as a promifed land, where I might lay in provifions
for the remainder of my journey : it was
ftill day light when we entered the town,
but we found it totally deferted, and we
had nothing to do but to enter the beft-
looking houfe among them, for they were
all open, which belonged to a Boyard ‡, as
my conductor told me. This fituation afforded us few refources ; I prevailed on my
guide,

‡ Boyard,—a Moldavian gentleman.

guide, however, to go, from me, to afk
affiftance from the fuperior of a neighbouring convent. I was waiting with impatience for his return, when a coach with fix
horfes appeared in the court-yard; it was
the mafter of the houfe. He told me on
entering, that informed by my emiffary of
the honour I had done him in taking up
my abode at his houfe, and hearing of my
wants, he was come that no other perfon
might have the fatisfaction of providing for
them. So polite an opening gave us frefh
hopes; and the arrival of provifions proved they were not ill-founded. However
confequential my hoft might appear, I foon
perceived that he was not the eagle of
the diftrict, and that giving way, from
feeblenefs of character, to every impulfe,
the laft fpeaker, with him, was always the
moft perfuafive orator; I confequently
found no difficulty in demonftrating to
him the danger to which the Boyards expofed themfelves, by not preventing the
inhabitants from quitting their houfes, and
even by fetting them the example. He
informed

informed me that all the inhabitants of the
town, to the number of feven or eight
thoufand, terrified at the bad treatment
and ravages of fome Sipahis, had taken refuge in the convent which I had fent to;
that feveral Boyards, as timid as the multitude, fomented this confufion, without
forefeeing the bad confequences. " I was
one of the number," added he, " but you
have made me change my opinion; come
with me and do the fame fervice to my
companions." The pleafure of bringing
back all thefe unfortunate people to their
habitations, who were threatened by no
immediate danger, made me infenfible to
the rifque of attempting this good work.
I kept my hoft all night, and, as my road
lay directly before the gate of the monaftery, the next morning the cries of the
women and children, the tumult of the
multitude crouded together, and the picture of the furrounding mifery, determined
me to follow my Boyard. He affifted me
in paffing through the croud to a flight of
fteps, on the top of which his companions
received

received me, and introduced me into the
hall, where they held their meetings. I,
had produced fuch an effect on my hoft,
that ftill full of my arguments, he was
willing to attempt the converfion of his
companions; but he was inftantly interrupted by the reproaches they fhowered
upon him, which confirmed me in my
opinion, that he at leaft was not the leader
of a party. I then thought it time to difplay my eloquence, but I foon perceived
that it would have no great fuccefs; my
audience was tumultuous, and the tumult
left very little interval to the calm I had
endeavoured to eftablifh. I next had re-
courfe to more efficacious meafures. A
panic had occafioned this diforder; a more
fubftantial terror appeared to me the only
remaining remedy. I changed my tone,
and threatened to complain to the Kam,
and to prevail on him to do fpeedy juftice.
I apologized for the people who always fuffer themfelves to be carried away by their
leaders; I accufed the perfons who liftened
to me, with rebellion, and from that moment

ment they appeared before me trembling
and fubmiffive. "Speak yourfelf, then,
to this frightened croud," fays the moft
turbulent of the Boyards; "you will prevail on them more readily than we can;
they will blefs you, and fo far from ac-
cufing us, you will be able to bear witnefs
to our good difpofition." This I evaded
a long time, and fhould never have accepted the dangerous part he propofed to me,
had I not perceived, on returning to the
fteps to go away, that it was impoffible to
get through the croud, who were in violent agitations of anxiety ever fince my arrival. "Speak to thefe unhappy people,"
repeats the fame Boyard to me, advancing
to the front of the fteps, to ferve me, no
doubt, as a colleague on this new tribune
of harangues. Three Janiffaries, armed
to the very teeth, were fitting there with all
the furlinefs of Iflanifm. Their confequential air convinced me they had protectors,
and feeing it neceffary to put an end to this
unpleafant adventure, I thought it beft to
begin by ftriking an awe into thefe bravoes,

in

in order to make an impreſſion on the multitude. " What are you doing here ?"
ſaid I, in a firm tone of voice ; " We are
defending theſe infidels," anſwered one of
them. " You are defending them," replied I, " againſt whom ? Who are their
enemies ? Is it the Grand Signior, or
the Kam of the Tartars ? In that caſe you
are rebels, and the ſole promoters of the
ſedition. Depend on it I will ſee you pu-
niſhed." Before I had finiſhed this ſhort
apoſtrophe, the inſolence of my Turks had
given place to fear ; they had got up to
liſten to me, and went down the ſteps ex-
culpating themſelves. This firſt advantage over the auxiliary troops had attract-
ed the attention of the croud, whoſe ſilence
appeared to me a good omen. I then advanced and raiſing my voice in Greek, I
was upon the point of obtaining all the ſuc-
ceſs of Demoſthenes, when a drunken fellow, puſhing through the croud, and
ſtanding forth as the champion of the ad-
verſe party, inſolently broke out into the
following diſcourſe :—" What do you
talk

talk of fubmiffion, of tranquillity, of cultivation, whilft we are dying with hunger?
Bring us fome bread," cried out this madman, " that is what we want."—" Aye,
bread," cried out the people in a fury.
Perceiving then my whole edifice overturned, and no means of extricating myfelf from the fituation in which I had fo
imprudently engaged, I took out of my
pocket two handfuls of money, that I had
of different kinds ; " There" cried I,
throwing it amongft the croud, " there
is bread for you, my good people ; return to your habitations, where you will
find abundance." The fcene quickly
changed ; one overturned another, to pick
up the money ; the drunken fellow difappeared amongft the combatants ; bene-
dictions fucceeded to abufe, and my defire
to make my efcape was at leaft equal to the
inconfiderate zeal which had brought me
amongft them. I received, however, all
the honours of war on my retreat, and re-
gained my carriage amidft the applaufes of
the people, who had opened a paffage for
me,

me, and next day returned to their habitations. My colleague, who was waiting for me at the gate of the convent, where I had been making my orations, was not without uneafinefs for the confequences of my imprudence. We were mutually very happy to meet together, and continued our journey daily, making the moft of the provifions with which the Boyard had fupplied us. The villages we paffed through, comprehended in the general devaftation of Moldavia, fcarcely afforded us a fhelter during the night. Wallachia, alfo, had been ravaged by fome Turks who were on their way to join the Kam; and who did nothing elfe, in fa& , but lay wafte their own country. There is no horror which thefe Turks did not perpetrate ; and, like a licentious foldiery, at the facking of a town, not content with difpofing of every thing at their fancy, ftill aimed at fucceffes the leaft to be defired. Some Sipahis ‡ carried their atrocity fo far, as to infult the perfon of the Old Rabbi of

‡ Turkifh Cavalry.

the

the Synagogue, and the Greek Archbi-
fhop.

We arrived at length at Kicherow, after
a great deal of fatigue, and very wretched
living ; but the Governor made us forget
every thing, by giving us an excellent
fupper, and good beds. We had now only
twelve leagues farther to go, and I had
given orders to be ready early in the morning ; when, on awakening, I was informed it was impoffible. After an exceffive
froft in the evening, there had fallen fo
great a quantity of fnow, that the road
acrofs the mountains was become impaffa-
ble for carriages. I was, however, by no
means difpofed to fubmit to the obftacles
which feemed to combine in retarding our
return to the Kam ; but my old Tartar,
lefs active, and more fatigued than I was,
agreed to ftay behind to take care of the
baggage. I fet out on a fledge, and the
rapidity of this conveyance foon brought
me into the plains of Kaouchan, where I
was ftill to encounter frefh difficulties. The
want of fnow, added to the moft complete
thaw,

thaw, was again very near ſtopping me,
had I not met with a cart, which ſuited
me very well ; but it was neceſſary to
make uſe of ſome violence with the owner,
to force him to conduct me. I was perch-
ed up with my Secretary on this carriage, and we were congratulating ourſelves on not arriving on foot, when, one
of the wheels breaking, we were at laſt
obliged to adopt this meaſure, which certainly did not add much to the dignity of
the return of the Ambaſſador of the Tartars.   I did not wait for my colleague,
whoſe return was delayed for ſome days,
to pay my compliments to the Kam.   He
was already informed of my curious entry
into Kaouchan ; and this Prince no ſooner
ſaw me, than he began with bantering me
on the modeſty of his Plenipotentiary.
Every thing I told him reſpecting Moldavia, ſeemed to him of ſo much importance, that he gave orders to remedy this
diſaſter, at the ſame time that he ſent intelligence of it to the Porte.   The inquiry into the cauſes, gave Krim-Gueray an
opportunity

opportunity of difclofing to me his opini-
nion of the Grand Vifir, *Emin Pacha.*
This Turk had begun his career as a fhop-
keeper's man, and in time attaining the
place of writer of the Treafury, he rofe
rapidly, by his intrigues, to the firft offices of the ftate. His prefumption made
him afpire at the Vifirate, on the declaration of war ; but his ignorance foon gave
his mafter reafon to repent of fo bad a
choice. The Vifir's faults could not efcape
the penetration of the Kam. He explained himfelf fully on the fubject, and was
contriving means to preferve the Ottoman empire from the confequences of
the folly and mifconduct of its Prime
Minifter.

The incurfion into New Servia, concerted at Conftantinople, was confented to in
the affembly of the grand vaffals of Tartary, and orders were expedited into all
the provinces, to claim the tribute of military fervice. *Three* horfemen were demanded from *eight* families, and this was
deemed fufficient to compleat the three armies, which were to begin their operations

at

at the fame time. That of the Nouradin, of 40,000 men, had orders to march
to the leffer Don ; that of the Calga, of
60,000, was to file along the left bank of
the Borifthenes, as far as Orela ; and the
main army, commanded by the Kam in
perfon, confifting of 100,000 men, was
deftined to penetrate into New Servia.
The troops of Yedeffan and Boudjak, were
peculiarly appropriated to this army, the
rendezvous general of which was fixed to
the neighbourhood of Tombachar.

On communicating to me all thefe particulars, Krim-Gueray afked me if I intended accompanying him on this expedition ? I anfwered him, that the honour
of refiding with him, on the part of the
Emperor of France, rendering it my duty
not to be diftant from his perfon, took
from me the merit of making a choice.—
" That title by which you are placed near
me," replied he, " is enough to make me
keep you. We are going to fuffer very fevere colds ; your drefs is not calculated for
them : drefs yourfelf in the Tartar fafhion;
—there

—there is no time to be loft;—we fhall fet out in about a week."—I rofe immedi-ately, to go and give orders for my cam-paign equipage, and was leaving the Prince's apartment, when the Mafter of the Ceremonies, followed by two Pages of the Chamber, cloathed me in a fuperb pelice, made of the neck of the white Lapland wolf, lined with light grey fur. I turned round to thank the Kam for the honour he did me. "It is a Tartar houfe I give you," faid he, laughing; "I have fuch a one myfelf, and I wifh us to wear the fame uniform."

The Grand Equerry fent me the fame day ten Circaffian horfes; advifing me, from his mafter, not to take my Arabian horfes into the field, which were neither able to withftand the cold, nor want of forage. But the fcantinefs of this fupply did not infpire me with much confidence; nor did I think proper to follow the ad-vice which accompanied the prefent.

Whilft my Tartar dreffes were making, I provided myfelf with three dromedaries, and

and ordered the neceffary tents to be got ready. Their mechanifm, as fimple, as it is eafy, merits defcription. Continually encamped, it is natural to fuppofe that the Tartars have carried that art to perfection. All their ideas are concentered in an object indifpenfably become their principal want. A nation at all times unacquainted with the luxury of indolence, muft neceffarily bend all its attention, and all its refearches towards that which is connected with bodily exercife, field fports, and warlike apparatus. The Tartars never take repofe but in their hours of leifure; they are fedentary, without effeminacy; and their camps are an exact counterpart of their ordinary habitations.

A lattice work, which eafily folds and unfolds, forms a fmall circular wall, four feet and a half high, the two extremities of which, two feet diftant from each other, form the entrance of the tent; after which, eighteen or twenty rods, joined at one end, and having a ring of leather at the other, to hook on to the crofs-bars of the

lattice

lattice work, form the pent of the dome, and fupport the covering of felt in the form of a cone, the circumference of whofe bafe covers the walls, which are lined alfo with the fame ftuff. This covering is bound with a girth, and a few fhovels full of fnow, thrown up againft the walls, prevents the external air from penetrating, and perfectly confolidates thefe tents, without either pofts or cordage.— Some of them, formed on a more refined plan, by applying a circular hoop at the top of the cone, to which all the rods are faftened, by leaving a paffage to the fmoke, admits of a fire in the tent, without rendering it more acceffible to the intemperance of the fevereft climate.

The tent of the Kam was of this kind, but fo large, that more than fixty perfons might conveniently fit round the wood fire. Decorated on the infide with a crimfon ftuff, it was furnifhed with a circular carpet, and fome cufhions. Twelve fmall tents, placed around that of the Prince, for the ufe of his officers and pages, were
contained

contained within an inclofure of felt, five feet high.

Every thing was prepared for taking the field; the troops of Bafs-Arabia, collected at Kichela, under the Sultan Serafker, waited only the fignal of departuie. It was fixed for the 7th of January, 1769, when Krim-Gueray began his march from Kaouchan, with the troops of his body-guard, the Sultans who had permiffion to follow him, his Minifters, his great officers, and all the volunteer Mirzas. The firft day was taken up in paffing the Neifter; eight rafts were prepared for this purpofe, on which the baggage had been paffed over the preceding evening. We found all the tents pitched alfo on the other fide. The firft care of the Kam was to enquire where mine were placed; and finding them too diftant from him, he gave orders that in future, they fhould be nearer his own. This Prince had defired me likewife to make no provifion, taking upon himfelf to furnifh me during the campaign. The 8th

was employed in paffing the Bafs-Arabian
troops.

I was that evening in the Kam's tent,
with fome Sultans of his fociety, when
his Vifir came to announce to him the arrival of a Lefgian Prince, brother to the
Sovereign of thefe Afiatic Tartars.   He
was invefted with the charaĉter of Ambaffador, to do homage to Krim-Gueray, and
to make him an offer of 30,000 men for
the prefent war.   I had the honour of affifting at his prefentation.   A fhort harangue, majeftically delivered, explained
the objeĉt of his miffion ; and the anfwer
of the Kam, accepting the homage, but
declining the proffered fuccours, reconci-
led at once the dignity of the Lord Paramount, and the confequence of the General.   The Ambaffador then folicited, and
obtained permiffion, to make the campaign.   This ceremonial finifhed, Krim-
Gueray invited his diftinguifhed gueft to
fupper.

If we may judge of a nation from an
Ambaffador of his high rank, and from
the

the perfons who accompanied him, we
muft form the moft advantageous opinion
of the Lefgian Tartars; all of them of a
great fize, and well proportioned, joined
to very noble countenances, an eafy carriage, and a military air. I muft obferve,
too, that their arms, fuch as are in ufe in
Europe, were perfectly well finifhed; and
I fhall add, on the teftimony of Krim-
Gueray himfelf, that his fpecimen by no
means exaggerates the appearance of the
whole body of the Lefgian troops. I have
reafon to believe alfo, that being in the vicinity of that nation, he would not have
refufed their offer, if the coaft of the Caf-
pian Sea, inhabited by this people, could
have been left defencelefs, without endangering the Cabarta.

The colds, which notwithftanding the
great falls of fnow, had not yet frozen the
Borifthenes, very foon became fo piercing,
as to allow the Tartars collected on the
other fide to pafs over on the ice. We
were encamped, and waiting for them near
Tombachar. I paffed my evenings with

I 2   Krim-

Krim-Gueray, whofe ideas, often original,
were always noble, and always exprefled
in the moft ftriking manner. This Prince
had effential need of giving a free fcope to
a philofophical turn of mind, which his
courtiers were not calculated to gratify.—
On this account our converfations became
the only remedy capable of diffipating thofe
hypochondriac affections to which he was
fubject. He took particular delight in in-
veftigating the prejudices which govern
different nations ; he amufed himfelf by
tracing up to their fources thefe prejudices,
to which he attributed every error, and
even almoft every crime ; and in bewailing
humanity, to vindicate its infirmities, con-
ftituted his philofophical amufement. It
is my duty to bear my teftimony to the talents and underftanding of this Prince :
I have feveral times heard him deliver his
opinions on the influence of the climate, on
the abufes and advantages of liberty, on
the principles of honour, on the laws and
maxims of a government, in a manner
which

which would have done honour to Mon-
tefquieu himfelf.

A great part of his troops were already
affembled, and the effect of the meafures
taken to victual the army during its ftay
at Balta, determined the Kam to proceed
thither. This town, fituated on the confines of Poland, and the fuburb of which
is in Tartary, became celebrated by the
commencement of hoftilities ; but at that
time, totally deftitute of inhabitants, prefented nothing but the moft frightful picture of devaftation. The 10,000 Sipahis
fent by the Turks to join the Tartars, had
reached this place before us ; and had not
only laid wafte Balta, but had burned alfo
all the neighbouring villages. Krim-Gueray led on, with regret, fuch wretched
and ill-difciplined troops ; he augured ill
of their courage, and acted only in defe-
rence to the good opinion the Grand Signior had formed of them. This body of
cavalry, accuftomed to the comforts and
inactivity of a long peace, no way formed
to fatigue, uninured to the cold, and fo ill-
cloathed

cloathed withal, as not to be able to withftand it, could be of no effectual fervice
whatever.   Their bravery was not lefs fufpected by the Kam of the Tartars, than are
in general their principles of religion.   It
is hard to know, in fact, whether the Arnaouts † Timoriots ‡ give the preference to
the Coran or the Gofpel.   I was returning
one night from the Kam's, in a Tartar
drefs, and was croffing the fquare of Balta,
to return to my lodgings; two Sipahis,
who were likewife returning home, walked
before me, converfing in Greek, curfing
their fituation, and fwearing by the *Holy
Crucifix* to revolt on the firft opportunity.
This excited my curiofity, to make them
explain the contradiction; and mending
my pace, I came up with them, giving
them the Mahometan falute, which they
very

† Under this name of Arnaouts, are comprehended
all the people of Turkey in Europe, which borders
on Sclavonia.
‡ Timoriots are the poffeffors of fiefs, held under
the Sovereign by military fervice; and the Timors
are particularly appropriated to the Sipahis, who
compofe the Turkifh cavalry.

very folemnly returned in the Turkiſh language; I then addreſſed them in Greek; —" Adieu! Brethren, we are no more Turks, one than the other of us." This adieu was not of a nature to ſeparate us ſo ſoon. Enchanted with me, they were only aſtoniſhed that a Tartar could be a Chriſtian; but not wiſhing to be known, I framed a ſtory. They confeſſed to me that they were only Mahometans for the *Timar*; and this was all I wanted to know.

The main army was collected, and the colds became ſo violent, that they left the field open for the Tartars to make their incurſions into New Servia. We had juſt been informed that the army under the Calga was aſcending towards the Samara; that the Nouradin's army was alſo on its march; and Krim-Gueray, after adapting his plans to this new information, quitted Balta to encamp near Olmar. This town, dependent on Tartary, had been partly burnt by the Sipahis, who completed its deſtruction even under the eyes of the Sovereign. To this outrage, they added

added the infolence of coming in a body to him, to demand barley for their horfes, whilft his own, as well as thofe of the whole army, were reduced to browze under the fnow. The indignation of the Kam was very near breaking forth into cruelty ; but he confined himfelf to menaces, forefeeing that this infolent banditti would foon be reduced by the cold to the moft complete fubmiffion.

Hitherto I had been fupplied by the Prince ; we ftill had frefh provifions, and I had not been in the way of judging of what was left for the remainder of the campaign ; but the fcarcity at the camp at Olmar, prepared us the firft truly military fupper. I was waiting for it without anxiety, but not without appetite, when the officers of the kitchen came to lay out the field table. It confifted of a round trencher of Ruffia leather, of about two feet diameter ; with this trencher were two bags, from whence they drew out fome excellent bifcuit, and fmoaked horfes ribs, the delicioufnefs of which was an inexhauftible

hauftible topic ; poutargue, cavear †, and
raifins, for the deffert, completed the
banquet. " How do you like the Tartar kitchen ?" fays the Kam, laughing ;
" Dreadful for your enemies," replied I.
A page, to whom he whifpered a moment
after, prefented me with the fame gold
cup made ufe of by his mafter. " Tafte
my drink, alfo," fays Krim-Gueray. It
was excellent Hungarian wine, which he
continued to favour me with the reft of
the campaign.

On the following days the army marched towards the *Bog*, which we croffed on
the ice, and eftablifhed our firft camp in
the Zaporovian Deferts. Notwithftanding the advice that had been given me, I
had amongft my horfes an Arabian, which
was very foon exhaufted, and, finking under the rigour of the climate, fell down to
die after the paffage of the river. The
animal had fcarcely any breath remaining,
when fome Noguais came to beg him of

I 5   me

---

† Poutargue and Cavear, are the fpawn of fifh
falted, but varioufly prepared.

me as a prefent. " What would you do,"
faid I, " with the dead horfe?"—" Nothing," fays one of them ; " but he is
not dead; we fhall be in time to kill him,
and to regale ourfelves on him, particularly as he is a white horfe, whofe flefh is
always the more delicate." I readily
granted them this morfel, to fatisfy their
appetite ; but I will not undertake to fay
that they arrived in time to fatisfy the
Muffulman law, in all its fcrupulous ex-
actnefs.

The cold, however, became fo exceffive,
and the plains we paffed over, which had
been lately burnt, afforded fo little pafturage, that after croffing _L'Eau Morte_ *,
(the Dead Water) a refolution was taken to
follow the courfe of that river, and to encamp amongft the reeds, which were difcovered by our patroles. We had need of
them to warm ourfelves, and to feed our
horfes ; but the Turkifh cavalry, who had
flattered themfelves, no doubt, with the
hopes of making war only with Polifh villages, being provided neither with tents

* A River in New Servia.

nor

nor provifions, experienced at once all the
feverity of cold and hunger : befides their
original want of forefight, they had the
imprudence, on their arrival at the camp,
to come near the fires; the greateft number of them, in confequence, were maimed, and pity very foon fucceeded the general indignation infpired by their rob-
beries and devaftation. The Kam, informed that thefe wretches were begging
their fubfiftence from tent to tent, ordered a certain portion of bifcuit to be collected from each Mirza, and diftributed
amongft them.

A fmall eminence we fell in with the
next day, whilft the army was marching
in line of battle, over an extenfive plain,
gave Krim-Gueray the defire of feeing all
his troops from it in one point of view.—
He ordered a halt : I followed him upon
this rifing ground ; and the dark colour of
the Tartarian drefs, contrafted with the
whitenefs of the fnow, which ferved as a
back-ground to the picture, fuffered nothing to efcape the eye. We diftinguifhed
by

by the ftandards, the troops of the refpective provinces; and I could not help
remarking, that without any fixed order,
the army had thrown itfelf naturally into
twenty files deep, and in lines tolerably
well formed. Each Sultan Serafker, with
his little court, formed an advanced groupe
before his divifion. The centre of the line,
occupied by the Sovereign, formed of itfelf a pretty confiderable advanced corps,
the arrangement of which formed a picture
no lefs military than agreeable. Forty
companies, each compofed of forty horfemen, four abreaft, led the van, in two
columns, and formed an avenue, lined on
each fide with twenty pair of colours.—
The G: and Equerry, followed by twelve
led horfes, and a covered fledge, marched
immediately after, and preceded the body
of horfe which furrounded the Kam. The
ftandard of the Prophet, borne by an Emir,
as well as the two pair of green colours
which accompany it, came next, and were
feen blended with the ftandard of the
Crofs, belonging to the troop of Inat Coffacks,

facks, attached to the Prince's body-guard,
which clofed the march.

This nation of the Inat Coffacks, which
is indebted for its poffeffions to the circumftances of its emigration from Ruffia, is
eftablifhed in the Cuban. One Ignatius,
more tenacious of his beard than of his liberty, to efcape from the razor of Peter
the Great, attended by a numerous fet of
followers, took refuge with the Kam.
The Tartars found fo much analogy between the word *Inat*, (opinionated) and
the word *Ignatius*, that they continue to
bear the former appellation, to mark the
motive of their emigration. They do not
appear to have preferved with the fame attention the purity of Chriftianity, but they
faithfully retain the fign of it on their
banners, and are ftill fcrupuloufly attached to the privilege of eating pork. Each
of our Inats had a quarter of fwine's flefh,
by way of portmanteau. The Turks, on
thefe occafions, muft find the Prophet's
ftandard in very bad company ; and I have
often heard them murmuring againft that

as

as a facrilegious profanation, which the
Tartars had the good fenfe to regard as a
matter of perfect indifference.

The reft of the army had not fo ftriking
an appearance of forefight.   Eight or ten
pounds of millet, roafted, pounded, and
preffed together, in a little bag of leather,
fufpended to the faddle of every Noguais,
furnifhed the army with a certain provifion for fifty days.   The horfes alone were
left to their own induftry to find fubfiftence ; but their prefent fituation differed
very little from that to which they had always been accuftomed.   The little attention their horfes require, induces the Tartars alfo to bring two or three, and often
more into the field, fo that we had more
than three hundred thoufand in the army.

The Kam, who was much pleafed with
what he had feen, afked the Sultans and
his Minifters, if in the view they had juft
taken, they diftinguifhed the braveft man
in the army? The filence of the courtiers
marked fufficiently their anfwer. " It is
neither you, nor I," refumed Krim-Gueray,
jocularly ;

jocularly; " we are all armed :—Tott is
the only man who dares go to war unarm-
ed; he has not even a knife." This pleafantry terminated the review; and the army refumed its march to the head of the
Eau Morte, where we did not arrive till
very late, and encamped in an immenfe
open fpace, lined with reeds.

For feveral days paft, Krim-Gueray had
been complaining of a pain in his thumb,
where an abfcefs was formed,and produced
a fever; *we had no furgeon with us :* I offered him my fervices, and the infpe𝔠tion
of a fet of lances I carried about me, in
cafe of need, determined him to truft me
with the operation. I immediately applied my inftrument; the incifion calmed
his pain, the fever difappeared, and the
wound, which was healed in a few days,
did me much honour, and afforded me
particular fatisfa𝔠tion.

From the time of our entering the Zaporovian plains, I never quitted the Kam's
tent, where we converfed together till
midnight. Wrapped up in his pelice, he
repofed

repofed-himfelf on a cufhion, and ordering
me to do the fame, two pages kept up a
good fire, which was very neceffary. But
if I wanted reft, he was not difpofed to
let me long enjoy it. This Prince was accuftomed to fleep only three hours, and I
with difficulty obtained five minutes ref-
pite, whilft the coffee was preparing.
Thus awakened, without changing my
place, I refumed the attitude of the preceding evening.

It was foon perceived that the tent of
the Kam was fituated on the ice; but nobody difcovered until day-break, and at
the moment of departure, that all the army had encamped upon a lake, the furface
of which, weakened by an infinite number of holes made in it to procure water,
threatened to fwallow up every thing. No
tent was left ftanding but the Kam's. I
was alone with him, when a Polifh foldier
in my retinue, rufhing in like a madman,
places himfelf near the fire, and begins
pulling off his cloaths; I ran to him, to
turn him out, thinking him either drunk

or

or mad, and threatened him with the difpleafure of the Kam.   Nothing moves
him; and I could only get a fign from
him to let him alone.   He had already
got off his boots, when Krim-Gueray perceived, by the cracking of his cloaths, that
he had fallen into the water, " What are
you going to do with the poor fellow?"
fays he to me, with goodnefs, " the man
who is dying, is he not independent? He
knows nobody but the perfon who can
affift him.—Kings are no longer any thing
for him!—Let us leave him the tent to
himfelf."—We went out; and I ordered
my people to take care of him.

The army, bending its courfe always to
the northward, endeavoured to approach
the Great Ingul, of the pofition of which
we had very vague ideas; but by a forced
march of twelve leagues, we at length encamped on the banks of that river: a few
deferted dwellings, and fome hay-ftacks
around them, were of effential fervice to
us.

We

We were now on the confines of New
Servia, and had reached the point from
whence our incurfions were to ftrike terror
into the wretched inhabitants ; and the
council of war was fummoned to felect the
troops neceffary for that expedition.
Whilft it was affembled, a meffenger, and
fome prifoners made by the patroles, depo-
fed that the Zaporovian Coffacks on our
right, menaced by the Caïga Sultan, having demanded and obtained a neutrality
of this Prince, had refufed to give any
affiftance to the Ruffian Governor-Gene-
ral of St. Elizabeth. Thefe particulars
made the Kam and his Generals acquainted with their true pofitions. It was refolved in confequence, that a third part of
the army, compofed of volunteers, under
the orders of a Sultan, and feveral Mirzas, fhould pafs the river at midnight,
divide itfelf into feveral columns, and fucceffively fub-dividing, fhould overrun
New Servia, burn all the villages and
crops which were gathered in, carry off
all the inhabitants, and drive off their cattle. It was befides determined, that each

foldier

foldier fhould have two affociates in that
part of the army which remained. By this
arrangement, every body was to partake
of the booty ; thus, avoiding all difcuf-
fions about fhares : and the general intereft concurred with that of individuals, to
make a good choice of the foldiers deftined for this expedition. The detachment was likewife apprized, that the remainder of the army, paffing the Ingul
the next day, would direct its courfe by
flow marches towards the frontiers of Poland, ftreightning St. Elizabeth, to pro-
tect the foragers, and wait for their return. The deftructive talents difplayed
fo eminently by the Sipahis on former occafions, feemed to difcover fo much zeal
for devaftation, that they were invited to
take a fhare in this expedition ; but the
cold had reduced them fo low, that none
of them were inclined to march. There
were only the Serdenguetchety §, and

§ A fort of Turkifh troops, whofe name fignifies
Forlorn Hope, volunteers determined to conquer or
to die ; but neither the one nor the other ever happens to them.

fome

fome other Turks who followed the Sultan.

The detachment under his orders had marched; and the cold, already lefs fevere than on the preceding evening, was fo diminifhed during the night, that a thaw was to be apprehended. The water even began to cover the ice on the river, and left us no hopes of being able to crofs it but by haftening our departure. The army was foon ready ; and extending itfelf along the Ingul, was put in motion at the fame moment. The Tartars, accuftomed to fuch expeditions, feparating themfelves at a certain diftance from each other, croffed it lightly, in a little trot ; but a number of the Sipahis, who trod heavily, from fear, and who were fo terrified by the noife of the broken ice, as to ftop fhort, and were fwallowed up before our eyes. We halted on the other fide of the river, to give time for the troops to form. Some Sipahis, who had efcaped from the danger, were deploring the fate of their comrades ; particularly

one

one of thefe poor wretches, whofe father had juft perifhed in the river, with a fum confiderable enough to have made his fortune. One of the Inat Coffacks immediately propofed to fifh up the purfe for two fequins ; his offer is accepted, and he undreffes himfelf, whilft they point out to him the hole amongft the flakes of ice ; he plunges in, and remains long enough under water to make the fpectators uneafy ; but after a few minutes, he appears with the treafure in his hand. This fuccefs encourages one of the comrades of the deceafed, who regrets his piftols mounted with filver ; the intrepid Coffack undertakes a fecond trip, fatisfies his defire, without difputing about an increafe of reward, receives his two fequins, puts on his cloaths, and runs to rejoin his colours.

In execution of the plan refolved on, the army remounted the hill, until it fell in with the track beaten in the fnow by the troops of the incurfion. We croffed this road near the place, where dividing itfelf

into

into feven branches, it formed a goofe's
foot, to the left of which we conftantly
directed our courfe, taking care never to
touch upon any of the fubdivifions we fucceffively fell in with, the fmalleft of
which were at length no more than paths
traced out by one or two horfemen.

The weather becoming rainy, obliged
the army to halt on the banks of the Adjemka, where it paffed the night. But
this thaw, which at firft had made us uneafy, was rapidly fucceeded by fo fevere a
froft, that it was with difficulty the tents
could be folded up. Small hail, violently
drifted by the wind, cut our faces, and
made the blood come out of the pores of
the nofe, and the breath freezing to the
whiſkers, formed ificles fo heavy, as to be
very painful. A great part of the Sipahis,
maimed in the preceding marches, perifhed on that day; the Tartars themfelves
fuffered very feverely, but nobody dared
to complain. Krim-Gueray, who fince
his indifpofition, went part of the way in
a covered fledge, amufed himfelf, during
this

this time, by afking me queftions concerning the Pope, comparing his fituation to
that of the Holy Father, and regretting
that he was not in his place. I took this
opportunity of repiefenting to him the ha-
vock the cold was making in his army,
and the danger of too long a march. " I
cannot make the weather better," faid he,
" but I can infpire them with courage to
fupport its feverity."—He calls immediately for a horfe, and conforming himfelf to
the cuftom which prohibits the Oriental
Sovereigns from wearing fhawls, fuch as
private perfons cover their heads with,
he braves the hoary frofts, and by his example obliges the Sultans, the Minifters,
and every perfon about him, to go uncovered. This act of vigour put a ftop to the
murmurs, and gave the Prince an opportunity of viewing the picture of thofe difafters which occafioned them. In fact,
we were lofing both men and horfes every
moment. We met with nothing in the
plains but frozen flocks ; and twenty columns of fmoke rifing in the horizon,
completed

completed the horror of the picture, by proclaiming to us the fires which were already ravaging New Servia †.

Falling in at length with fome briars, and a little forage, the Kam determined to make a halt. His tent was pitched near a hay-ftack, which he ordered to be diftributed, and which, in fpite of its enormous fize, difappeared in an inftant. We amufed ourfelves with this fpectacle, which prefented at once the eagernefs of pillage, and the feverity of good difcipline. A meffenger from the Sultan who commanded the incurfion, brought us news in the evening from that Prince. He informed us that the inhabitants of a large village, having to the number of 1200, taken refuge in a Monaftery, had compelled him, by their refiftance, to fhoot off fome arrows with brimftone matches, in hopes of feeing their obftinacy give way to the fear of fire ; but that the conflagration, too rapidly furrounding thefe unfortunate peo-

† This day's march coft the army more than 3000 men, and 30,000 horfes, who perifhed by the cold.

ple,

ple, hadconfumed them all. The Sultan added to the deep regret he expreffed for this dreadful misfortune, fome complaints of the cruelty of the Turks who had accompanied him, whofe only courage, he faid, confifted in bathing themfelves in the blood of the prifoners.

Krim-Gueray was not lefs fenfible than the Sultan to the melancholy confequences of the conflagration ; the cruelty of the Turks filled him with indignation ; the fight of the heads cut off, ftill further fhocked him ‡. " I would hang up a Tartar," added he, " who fhould dare to prefent himfelf before me in the attitude of an executioner.—How can there exift fo ferocious a people as to encourage barbarity by rewarding it, and can take a pleafure in fuch difgufting objects ?"

The fucceffive arrival of the Tartars, who were already returning, laden with

‡ The Turks are accuftomed to carry the heads of their flain enemies to the General who commands them ; the Tartarson the contrary, hold this cuftom in abhorrence.

booty,

booty, and bringing us frefh particulars, had kept us awake till three in the morning. The entrance of the ·Kam's tent could not be fhut, under the prefent cir-cumftances, and ·I obtained permiffion to go and take fome hours reft in my own.— It was occupied by Meffrs. Rufin and Con-ftillier, who were half frozen, flept little, and were dying with hunger. A hard fnow formed the bed I came to fhare with them, and on which, wrapped up in my pelice, I took my place, and fell afleep. Soon after, one of the Kam's pages half opens the door, announces a prefent from his mafter, places it at the feet of Mr. Ru-fin, and withdraws. Mr. Conftillier, who was kept more awake by hunger, made no doubt but that it was fomething eat-able ; he knew alfo that I kept nothing concealed from him of that fort ; but too far off to examine the packet, he defires his companion to fee what it is ; who, on account of the fevere cold, refufes a long time : obliged, at length, to fubmit, he puts out his arm, keeping his head ftill covered

covered with his pelice, gets hold of fomething hairy, which he lifts up by the glim-
mering of a lamp hanging from the top
of the tent, and prefented to the greedy
eye of Mr. Conftillier a human face.
Struck with this horrible object, he cries
out,—" My friend, it is a head !" and
Mr. Rufin fent it as quick as lightning out
of the tent, both of them curfing the cold,
their hunger, and the Tartar pleafantries.

The cold increafed fo much next day,
that at our fetting out, notwithftanding
my gloves lined with hare fkin, my hands
were benumbed with it at the moment
of getting on my faddle, and I had much
difficulty to recover the circulation. The
columns of fmoke which covered the
horizon on the right, and Fort St. Elizabeth, which we perceived on our left,
left no longer any doubt about the route
we were to purfue ; we directed it towards
fome edifices in our front, which we foon
difcovered to be a preparation for fignals
of fire. Thefe triangular wooden frames,
eight ftories high, filled with ftraw and

faggots.

faggots, were, doubtlefs, intended to
fpread the alarm, on the firft appearance
of the Tartars; but they eventually ferved
only as guides for their army as far as
Adjemka. This town, preferved from
the ravages of the incurfion by its vicinity
to St. Elizabeth, contained only a few
inhabitants, and we fufpected that the
greateft part of them had taken refuge
under the cannon of that fortrefs.

The main army was in fo bad a ftate,
that it had every thing to fear itfelf from a
fally; in fact, two or three thoufand men
attacking it in the night, would only have
had the trouble of cutting us to pieces.
This danger was not more clearly proved,
than the impoffibility of avoiding it by
continuing a march, the fatigues of which
the troops were no longer able to fupport.
In this extremity, Krim-Gueray ordered
the Sultans, and the Mirzas to form a detachment of 300 horfemen, to go at fun-
fet to infult St. Elizabeth, in order to keep
the garrifon on the defenfive. This chofen
band, the only part of the army whofe
energy of mind was ftill able to furmount
the

the natural faintnefs arifing from a compli-
cation of fufferings, pufhing into the fuburb to make prifoners, made the fuccefs of
this military ftratagem fo complete, that
the army was enabled to ftay and recover
its fatigues in the midft of the greateft
plenty. The town of Adjemka, confifting of eight or nine hundred families, fituated on a fmall river of that name, proved
the fertility of its foil, by the abundance
of the crops of every kind. The troops,
however, were not allowed to occupy the
houfes, from fear of a premature conflagration. They were only permitted to
carry off the wood and provifions for confumption ; the Kam himfelf fet the example, by continuing under his tent. The
next day's reft, by recruiting their
ftrength, and giving time for a part of the
incurfion troops to join us with a vaft
number of flaves and cattle, diffufed a
general gaiety throughout the army.

I obferved that the Tartars of each hord,
and of each troop, had a watch-word to
which their comrades anfwered, to direct
them.

them. That of Ak-Seraï, *the White Palace*, was peculiar to the Kam's houfhold ; but if it be eafy to conceive the utility of this expedient, a circumftance one would fcarcely believe on feeing it, is the care, the attention, the patience, the extreme agility of the Tartars in keeping what they have taken. Five or fix flaves, of different ages, fixty fheep, and twenty oxen, the prize of a fingle man, do not embarrafs him. The children, with their heads peeping out of a fack, hanging by the pummel of the faddle ; a young girl fitting before, leaning on her left hand ; the mother behind on the crupper, the father on a led horfe, the fon upon another, fheep and oxen before them, every thing in a march, and nothing goes aftray from under the vigilant eye of the fhepherd of this flock. To collect, to conduct them, to provide for their fubfiftence, to go on foot to eafe his flaves, no trouble is too great for him ; and this fcene would be truly interefting, did not avarice, and the moft cruel injuftice, furnifh the fubject of the picture.

picture. I had gone out with the Kam to
view this fpectacle, when an officer of the
guard, which formed a line of circumval-
lation around the tent, came to acquaint
him, that a Noguais afked permiffion to
make a complaint to him. Krim-Gueray
confented ; and the Noguais, followed by
the fame officer, advanced towards us ;
but uncertain, from the fimilitude of our
pelices, to which of the two he fhould addrefs himfelf, he appears difpofed to give
the preference to me. I was going, however, to retreat, to put an end to his embarraffment, but the Kam, who had obferved it, making a fign to the officer to
let him remain in his error, drew back
himfelf, and ordered me to hear what he
had to fay. The cafe was a horfe which
had been loft, and of another which he
had ftolen in return, without being able
to juftify his pretended right of reprifal.
" What muft I anfwer ?" fays I, to the
Kam ; " Decide as you think proper,"
replied he, laughing. I pronounced, accordingly, the reftitution of the horfe
ftolen ;

ftolen ; and was about to difmifs the parties, when Krim-Gueray, who was amufing himfelf with this pleafantry, whifpers
me in the ear, not to forget the baftinado.
I immediately added, " I *pardon* thee the
baftinado thou haft merited." A fign from
the Kam, to carry my fentence into execution, proved to me that he was not dif-
pleafed at my mitigating his.

Every refearch that could be made after
the inhabitants of Adjemka, had hitherto
proved ineffeƈtual ; and it was not until
two days after, at the moment of our departure, on fetting fire to fome ftacks of
corn and forage, which concealed thefe
unfortunate people, that they came and
threw themfelves into the arms of their
enemies, to efcape the flames which were
deftroying their crops, and their habitations. The order to burn Adjemka, was
executed with fuch precipitation, and the
fire caught all the thatched houfes with
fuch violence and rapidity, that we could
barely efcape ourfelves through the flames.
The atmofphere, loaded with afhes, and
vapour

vapour of the melted fnow, after fome
time darkening the fun, formed, from the
combination of thefe different materials, a
greyifh fhower of fnow, which crafhed
between the teeth.. One hundred and
fifty villages, which were alfo confumed,
producing the fame effect, extended this
cloud of cinders full twenty leagues into
Poland, where our arrival would alone
furnifh the folution of this phœnomenon.
The army marched for fo long a time in
this obfcurity, that feveral hours elapfed
before we difcovered the defertion of a
large part of the Noguais of Yedefan,
who, being already joined by their foragers, were returning, at every hazard,
by the Defert, to avoid the ten per cent.
on their prizes, payable to their Sovereign.

The route of the army lying towards the
frontiers of the Polifh Ukraine, brought
the army to Crafnikow. This village,
fituated behind a marfhy ravine, contained
a fort of redoubt, in which the inhabitants, affifted by about a hundred foldiers,
at firft made fome refiftance ; but their

dread

dread of the flames foon obliged them to fly into a neighbouring wood, from whence they might annoy our troops with muf-quetry, even in the village. To diflodge them, Krim-Gueray, who went to the head of the wood in perfon, ordered the Sipahis, who were ftill remaining, to be-gin the attack. But thofe brave fellows, whom the ftay at Adjemka, and the inter-miflion of the cold had again rendered in-folent, were difperfed on the firft fire. The Inat Coffacks, drawn up behind us, ani-mated by the prefence of the Sovereign, demanded, and obtained permiflion to at-tack. Difmounting in an inftant, they penetrate into the wood, hem in the party who defend themfelves, kill about forty of them, and make prifoners of all thofe who were unable to efcape. During this expedition, which only coft the Coffacks eight or ten men, and a few flight wounds received by the Tartars, who were near the Kam, that Prince, fired with indigna-tion at the cowardice of the Turks, was converfing with me on the fubject, and predicting

predicting the humiliation which it muft
neceffarily bring upon the Ottoman empire.

Occupied with this idea, he was ftill on
horfeback at the entrance of the village,
when he perceived a Turk, of the race of
Emirs, who was coming on foot from the
wood, carrying a head in his hand. "Look
at that rafcal," faid he ; "he is coming
to fpoil my fupper ; but obferve him well;
he dares fcarcely touch the head, now that
he has cut it off." The Emir arrives ;
throws his trophy at the feet of the
Prince's horfe, and pronounces, with em-
phafis, his wifhes, "That all the enemies
of the Emperor of the Tartars, may fuffer
the fame fate as the one he has juft been
deftroying." Krim-Gueray, however, had,
by this time, difcovered in this head, the
features of one of his own Coffacks.—
"Wretch!" fays he, to the Emir, "how
did'ft thou kill him? Dead as he is, thou
art afraid of him; living, he would have
eat thee! It is one of my Inats, killed at
the attack of the wood: Who helped thee
to cut off his head—to affift thee in deceiv-
ing

ing me ? Thou wouldeſt not thyſelf, have had the courage!" The Turk, diſconcerted, ſtrives to defend himſelf; he inſiſts, and has the hardineſs to aſſert, that he killed the man himſelf, and that he was an enemy. " Examine his arms, then," ſays the Prince;—knife, ſabre, piſtols, every thing was examined on the ſpot, but nothing indicated that he had killed him. " Knock down this pretended man of courage," cries Krim-Gueray. An officer of the guard, giving him a ſlight ſtroke with his whip, was deſirous of ſparing the wretch, at the ſame time that he ſatisfied his maſter's anger. But the Turk, proud of his rank of Emir, the ſole privilege of which, in Turkey, is never more than reſpectfully to take off the head dreſs of the perſon to be beaten, exclaims with inſolence againſt this aſſault upon his perſon. The fury of the Kam could no longer be reſtrained: " Cut the green turban, with your whips, upon the raſcal's head!" This order, pronounced in a firm tone of voice, which allowed of no further palliation, was

executed

executed with a feverity more cruel than
death itfelf. This execution had a great
effect on the Sipahis, who, after refufing
to fhare with the Tartars in the fatigues of
the incurfion, ufed to watch their return,
and frequently rob them, with piftols at
their heads, of the flaves they were bringing back; and, after dragging thefe
wretched people about with them for
fome time, tired of the trouble, cut them
in pieces, to get rid of them.

The Kam propofed attacking the little
town of Sibiloff, fituated behind the wood,
at about a league and a half diftant from
us, the next morning; but from the report
of prifoners, the garrifon appearing too
ftrong for him to carry it, without cannon, he only permitted fome volunteers to
go there, whilft he, at the head of his army, bent his courfe towards Bourky, in
Poland.—The cannon of Sibiloff, which
we heard on our march, could not hinder
the Tartar detachment from burning the
fuburbs, and making a great number of
flaves. All the villages in our line of
march

march underwent the fame fate; and the
Tartars, more difpofed to get poffeffion of
the perfons of the inhabitants, than to ftu-
dy diftinctions refpecting the boundaries
of Poland, continued their ravages far beyond the prefcribed limits. But although
the orders of the Kam could not, at firft,
check the avidity of the Tartars, which
purpofely confounded the inhabitants of
New Servia with thofe of the Polifh Ukraine, the meafures adopted by the Prince
at length produced the defired effect; befides that, punifhment always very nearly
followed the offence.

To infure the refpect due to the Republic of Poland, the main body of the army
always encamped in the environs of the
villages, living on their own provifions;
and the Turks, for whom it was abfo-
lutely neceffary to procure lodgings, having dared to fet fire to fome houfes, were
feverely punifhed. A rough calculation of
the flaves carried off by the army, amount-
ed to 20,000: the cattle were innumera-
ble. We could only proceed by flow
marches;

marches; and the neceffity of watching
the conduct of the Tartars, determined
Krim-Gueray to march in feven columns.
In every village where we halted, our
lodgings, marked with chalk, left the Sipahis the choice of fuch houfes as were not
occupied by the Kam, and his attendants.
The Prince had given orders that mine
fhould be always near his. I enjoyed this
advantage very quietly for feveral· days,
until an Alay-Bey *, who, doubtlefs, had
not been able to find apartments in the
town worthy to receive him, very gravely
enters my lodgings, followed by two Sipahis, carrying his baggage. I afk him what
he wants ?—" Don't difturb yourfelf,"
fays he, coolly, and feats himfelf on a fort
of eftrade, between two cufhions, which
he never quitted, and afks for his pipe.—
In vain did I obferve to him that thefe
lodgings were defigned for me; that we
could not both occupy them; that I could
not be far from the Sovereign, nor he from
his troop. No argument has any weight
with

* Colonel of the Arnaout Sipahis.

with him ; he has taken up his quarters,
and is immoveable. I had no other re-
fource than to apply to the Seli&ar to free
me from this difagreeable intruder. The
Seli&ar comes immediately, under pre-
tence of paying me a vifit, and afks the
Colonel, on entering, how long he has
been acquainted with me ? The other, not
at all difconcerted, replies, that he is come
to make acquaintance with me, by lodg-
ing there. " It was at the attack of the
wood," fays the Captain of the Guards,
ironically, " that you fhould have made
acquaintance with us; we fhould then have
received you very cordially; but to-day,
you muft withdraw:—and, take my ad-
vice, not to wait until the Kam, informed of your conduA, makes you feel his
difpleafure."—" I know," replies the officer, " all his power ;—to take off my
head ;—he has only to fay the word;—he
may do that, if he pleafes ; but I will never go out of this houfe alive, before the
army marches."—This was his definitive
refolution, and nothing could fhake him.

Enraged

Enraged at this madman, the Selictar quitted me, to inform Krim-Gueray of what
had paffed.—I immediately received an invitation to wait upon him; and I found
him giving fuch orders as made me trem-
ble. Long irritated againft the cowardice
and bad difcipline of the Turks, the infolence of my Alay-Bey exhaufted his patience. I was only fent for, in fact, to
give him an opportunity of ftriking the
intended blow. The Kam was inclined to
extend his rigour to the whole body of
Sipahis, and could only be reftrained by
the fear of lying under the imputation of
prejudice. Whilft he was hefitating in
this refpect, I was determined to do every
thing in my power to leave the Colonel
quiet, whofe motto certainly was not—
' To *conquer*, or to die ;'—but, ' To *fleep*,
or die.' I urged, that my complaint might
have been improperly explained ;—that I
was the perfon to be heard ;—and having, at length, fucceeded in amufing the
Kam with remarks on the ridiculous obftinacy of the Arnaouts, I made my particular inftance difappear under the general
obfervation.

obfervation. The order was revoked, with
the obliging condition that I fhould no
more quit his tent.

The army laden with the plunder of
New Servia, regulating its march by that
of the cattle, was flowly approaching the
frontiers ; and the Tartars, always infatiable, were taken up with various attempts
to elude the vigilance of the Kam, in order
to increafe their booty, by marauding,
when it was ftrictly prohibited, under pain
of the fevereft punifhment. The dark
colour, however, of the Tartar drefs was
too eafily diftinguifhable at a diftance on
the fnow, to favour the ftratagems of the
plunderers. Some Noguais were detached
to turn a Polifh village, behind which
they were about to conceal themfelves,
when the Kam, paffing along the edge of
a wood, on a flat piece of ground, which
overlooked the plain, difcovered fome of
thefe marauders. He gave immediate orders to his Selictar to go in perfon, with
four Seimens, to fcour the village, and
bring him fuch of the Noguais as he fhould
find

find in the fact of plundering. The gloomy air with which Krim-Gueray gave this order announced an intended example.— Already did the Seliĉtar, who went full fpeed to the fpot, to execute his orders, make his appearance, bringing back with him a Noguais, and a piece of linen, and a couple of handfuls of wool, which he had taken. Interrogated by his Sovereign, the marauder confeffes his faults, admits that he was acquainted with the rigour of the orders againft this rapine, offers nothing in his defence, afks no favour, tries to intereft nobody in his behalf, and coolly awaits his fentence, without difplaying either infolence or weaknefs. " Let him difmount, and tie him to a horfe's tail, to be dragged until he dies ; and let a crier, following him, inform the army of the crime which has incurred this punifh-ment." To this dreadful fentence pronounced by the Kam, the Noguais makes no other reply than by difmounting from his horfe, and approaching the Seimens who were to bind him ; but there were
neither

neither cords nor ftraps. Whilft they were
looking for them, I attempt a word in his
favour; Krim-Gueray's only anfwer was
by fharply commanding them to put an
end to the bufinefs, by making ufe of a bow-
ftring.   They tell him it is too fhort.
" Well, let him pafs his head, then, through
the bow when it is bent."   The Noguais
obeys; follows the horfeman, who drags
him rapidly along, until, unable to keep
pace with the trot of the horfe, he falls,
and thus efcapes from the yoke by which
he is held.   A frefh order from the Prince
remedies this deficiency.—" Let him hold
the bow with his hands," added he.   The
criminal immediately croffes his arms, and
takes hold of it; and the complete execution of this fentence, which condemned
the prifoner to be his own executioner, affords, undoubtedly, an example of the
moft extraordinary fubmiffion; it furpaffes
all the ftrange ftories which have been
related of the blind obedience to the orders of the Old man of the Mountain §.
                                    The

§ Mr. Rufin, who accompanied me, and who is
                                    at

The attention of Krim-Gueray to the maintenance of good order in Poland, extended even to the religious worſhip of the inhabitants ; and ſome Noguais, convicted of having mutilated a picture repreſenting Chriſt, received a hundred ſtrokes of the baſtinado, at the gate of the church. " We muſt teach the Tartars," ſaid he, " to reſpect the fine arts and the Prophets."

Savran ‖ was now the deſired point, in which town the diſtribution of the booty was to take place ; the different hords were to be diſmiſſed, reſerving only the troops of Bafs-Arabia, and where we were to be freed from the rabble which ſurrounded us. It was determined to remain there, and the diviſion of the ſpoils was proceeded on the day after our arrival ; but the ſtricteſt attention could not prevent ſome rogues from getting their booty out of the way of the ten *per cent.* duty, payable to the Sovereign. But, notwithſtanding the frauds, the

at preſent Profeſſor in the Royal Academy at Paris, was, as well as myſelf, a witneſs to this incredible fact.

‖ A town in Poland, in the Palatinate of Bruklaw.

the Prince ftill received for his fhare near two thoufand flaves, which he made pre-fents of to the firft comer. I was necef-farily prefent at thefe tranfactions, and perceiving the liberality of the Kam in this particular, I reprefented to him, that if he continued, he would foon dry up the fource of it.

Krim-Gueray.

There will always be enough left for me, my friend; the age of defire is paft; but I have not forgot you: far from your *ha-rem*, marching over deferts, and braving the rigour of the climate with us, it is but juft that you fhould have your fhare. I defign for you fix *beautiful young boys*; fuch, in fhort, as I fhould make choice of for myfelf.

Baron.

I am overcome with your bounty; but can one be worthy of a favour, without feeling all its value? I fhould be afraid of not holding this prefent in fo much eftima-tion as you feem to do.

Krim-

Krim-Gueray.

It is by no means my wifh to bargain for your gratitude : I make you a prefent of thefe flaves ; they will give you pleafure, and that is all I defire.

Baron.

But, your ferenity overlooks my fituation, which forms an infurmountable obftacle to my accepting them. Your flaves are all Ruffians: How can I accept, as flaves, the fubjects of a power in friendfhip with the Emperor my mafter?

Krim-Gueray.

That reafon moft certainly efcaped me ; nor can I even conceive the principle on which it is founded. Hoftility makes flaves; friendfhip gives, and receives them: What have you to do with any thing elfe? I do not wifh, however, to difcufs your duty : it is your bufinefs to fulfil it ; and, to accommodate this matter between us, I will fubftitute fix young Georgians, in place of the fix Ruffians ; that affair is fettled.

Baron.

Baron.

Not fo eafily as you imagine, Sir ; I have ftill another intrenchment, difficult to force.

Krim-Gueray.

What is that ?

Baron.

My religion.

Krim-Gueray.

As for that fubject, I fhall take fpecial care not to touch on it. You do very well, doubtlefs, to conform to it ; but admit, at leaft, that it is very hard.

Baron.

I will do more ; I will confefs that human weaknefs very frequently goes aftray ; for example, it is very poffible that I only fhow myfelf fo fcrupulous, and fo attached to my duty, to-day, becaufe you offer me nothing which tempts me to deviate from it ; fix *pretty girls,* perhaps, might have made me forget all my principles ; and, if we examine, with attention, we fhall often find, that the moft fublime efforts

forts of virtue depend folely on the nature of the temptation.

Krim-Gueray.

That I perfectly comprehend; and that method of feduction would not have efcaped me, had it been in my power to employ it; but I, too, have my religion, my friend, which allows me to give *male* flaves to Chriftians, and enjoins me to keep the *females*, to make profelytes of them.

Baron.

You think it of lefs confequence, then, to make male than female converts?

Krim-Gueray.

Not at all; our great Prophet has forefeen every thing : this very diftinction proves it.

Baron.

I muft confefs that I do not perceive the difference; you will permit me, therefore, fimply to believe, that you are better pleafed with *pretty girls*.

Krim-Gueray.

No, I affure you ; but I act in obedience to a law, founded on reafon. Man, in

VOL. II.   L   fact,

fact, being from his nature independent, even in the state of slavery, retains a secret elasticity, which can hardly be restrained by fear ; he feels his powers, and is governed by his moral sense: God alone can influence his mind ; in your country, in mine, he may be equally enlighted ; the conversion of man is at all times a miracle ; that of a woman, on the contrary, is the most natural, and the most simple affair in the world : women are always of the religion of their lovers. Yes, my friend, love is the great missionary ; when he appears, there is an end to every dispute.

Nor did I dispute any longer this strange position, which is only applicable, doubtless, to women in a state of slavery.

After distributing the greatest part of the slaves which had fallen to his share, and sent off the Noguais, the Kam directed his march towards Bender ; but if the diminution of the army disencumbered us on our march, the Prince's generosity threw a fresh impediment in the way of so speedy a return as he desired. In fact, the

Sultans,

Sultans, and the Minifters, reduced, here-
tofore, to their camp equipage, now poffeffed, from their mafter's liberality, a fu-
perfluity, which prevented them from
marching with fo much celerity. The
Kadi-Lefker, the moft infatiable, as well
as the moft artful in pufhing his pretenfions, was confequently poffeffed of the
greateft fhare of the plunder. Curious to
examine his proceedings in the midft of
his abundance, I went one evening to fee
him.

This great Judge, venerable from his
age, and the whitenefs of his beard, care-
lefsly ftretched on the carpet, deftined for
the five prayers, was very differently employed; he was at that moment contem-
plating with a greedy eye, and a malicious
fmile, forty or fifty flaves, of different
ages; who, collected round a ftove, formed a groupe of figures of both fexes, all
with their eyes fixed on him. "I wifh you
joy," faid I, on entering, "of the fuccefs of a war by which, it feems, you have
been a confiderable gainer."

The

The Kadi-Lefker.

You fee, indeed, that the Kam has treated me handfomely ; but you know, likewife, that one muft be poffeffed of his
riches, to enjoy what he has given me.

Baron.

On the Kam's principles, however, refpecting the converfion of the women, he
has reckoned upon you, I imagine, to
make fome profelytes.

The Kadi-Lefker.

I was examining, when you came in,
which of thefe faces is the handfomeft.
Do you take a look, and fee if we fhall
agree in our choice.

Baron.

I have already made mine. That pretty
girl, ftanding on that bench, with her
flender fhape, her modeft air, and her foft
looks, has my vote.

The Kadi-Lefker.

For my part, I prefer that round face,
full of colour ; and I will anfwer for it,
that the little rogue will be charming in a
page's drefs. I own to you, that the flender
make

make with which you are captivated,
ftrikes me only as a want of *em bon point*.

Baron.

In that cafe, I am no longer forry for
you, for fhe is the only one who can be
reproached with that fault; but I fee there
fome very young ones; can you tell me at
what age one begins to *convert* them; and
if the Noguais, whofe activity in carrying
off girls I have been witnefs to, are not in
too great hafte to marry them?

The Kadi-Lefker.

No; the Tartars, on the contrary, are
very fcrupulous in that refpect.

Baron.

But fcrupulous as they are, Sir, they
cannot interrogate their flaves about their
age, and even that knowledge would be
infufficient.

The Kadi-Lefker.

They have a better method of quieting
their confciences. I'll tell you what it is:
if they are in doubt about the ftrength of
a young girl, they pretend to be out of
humour, terrify her, and oblige her to fave
herfelf

herfelf by flight ; and when fhe begins to run, they throw one of their caps at her, the fhock of which, without hurting her, is fufficient to make her fall, if fhe be weak ; in this cafe they refpect her extreme youth, comfort her for the fall, and wait patiently till fhe is ftrong enough to withftand this proof.

Baron.

I doubt much, whether that be fufficient ; but even in that cafe, can you always anfwer for the good faith of thofe who make ufe of it ? " You may always rely upon it," replied the Kadi-Lefker, " that their cuftoms are more faithfully obferved by a people whofe manners are fimple, than the moft rigorous laws are amongft polifhed nations."

A fort of indifpofition, which I felt at that moment, and which I attributed to the fuffocating heat in the chamber of the Kadi-Lefker, determined me to return home ; but the fudden tranfition from fuch an atmofphere, to a very piercing cold, affected me fo violently, that I fell down

fenfelefs

fenfelefs on the fnow. I lay there fome
time before one of the Judge's attendants
perceiving me, acquainted his mafter with
it. The affiftance, however, I received
from them would have done but little, had
not Krim-Gueray, informed of my acci-
dent, fent fome *eau de luce* by one of his
pages, which made me refpire. Notwithftanding this aid, I was too feeble to walk
home ; four Tartars carried me, and the
concern with which it affected Meffrs. Rufin and Conftillier, by awakening my fenfibility, affifted in recruiting my fpirits.

We arrived next day at Bender, and the
Governor came to meet us at fome diftance
from the town. At the Kam's approach,
this Vifir, followed by a great retinue, gets
from his horfe, with his whole troop, ad-
vances towards the Prince, falutes him
profoundly, and turns round to march on
foot before ; but this mark of refpect paid,
he received permiffion, from Krim-Gueray,
to mount and accompany him to the Niefter, which feparated us from the fortrefs.
There we perceived a bridge of boats,
which

which the Pacha had built with great difficulty, being obliged to break the ice
which covered the river ; but all thefe attempts to pay his court to the Tartar Sovereign were unfuccefsful ; nor could all the
arguments of the Vifir, prevail on the Prince
to pafs the bridge. " I crofs rivers," fays
he, " in a more œconomical manner."
This was no fooner faid, than putting his
horfe into a trot, he forces the Pacha, who
trembled at this pleafantry, to follow his
example. The cracking of the ice, which
broke under us, was indeed enough to
make him regret his pontoons ; and the
Kam's arguments of their inutility, had
no weight with him till he was fafely
landed on the oppofite fhore. During this
paffage, the cannon of the place had begun
the falute, and Krim-Gueray entered
Bender under a general difcharge of artillery. He was lodged at the Governor's,
and he here difmiffed the remainder of his
troops, whilft his houfhold went on to
Kaouchan, to prepare for his reception ;
and where we all arrived, well fatisfied
with

with the profpect of repofing ourfelves after the fatigues of the campaign.

The news, however, we received from Conftantinople, from whence the Ottoman army was preparing to begin its march towards the Danube, did not promife the Tartars any long inaction. In the midft of the pleafures by which Krim-Gueray delighted to unbend his mind, his forefight would not allow him to overlook the neceffary orders for collecting frefh troops, and he thought it neceffary to move himfelf towards Kotchim, that the Grand Vifir might be obliged to keep at a diftance; and, in fact, the ignorance which uniformly guided this Prime Minifter, ftood in need of being counteracted by a man fo powerful, and fo enlightened as the Kam, who was not, as we have already feen, too favourably difpofed towards Emin Pacha. The latter, more circumfpect in his difcontent, and forced to hide the means of manifefting it, was, on that account only, a more dangerous enemy.

L 5
In

In the midſt of theſe occupations, Krim Gueray had more frequent returns of thoſe hypochondriac complaints to which he was ſubjeƈt. Being alone with him during one of theſe attacks, which he ſupported with impatience, I was ſtriving to diſſuade him from the uſe of empyric remedies, when one *Siropolo*, who had already propoſed one to him, entered his apartment. This man, born at Corfu, by religion a Greek, a great chymiſt, phyſician to the Prince of Wallachia, and his agent in Tartary, had, in right of theſe titles, a free admiſſion to the Kam ; he did not let ſlip this opportunity of offering the ſuccour of his art, aſ-ſuring him, that one draught, by no means diſagreeable to the palate, would be ſuffici-ent to effeƈt a radical cure. " On thoſe terms I conſent," replied the Prince, and the doƈtor went out to comply with them. I ſhewed my uneaſineſs ſo plainly, that Krim-Gueray, taking notice of it, ſays to me, ſmiling, " What, my friend, you are afraid ?"—" Undoubtedly," replied I ſharply; " refleƈt on that man's ſituation, and

and your own, and judge whether I am
wrong." " What nonfenfe !" faid he ;
" what good can I derive from fuch an
examination ? A fingle glance is fufficient :
look at him—look at me, and fee whether
the infidel would dare !" In vain, did I make
ufe of the ftrongeft reprefentations, until
the phyfic arrived ; and the quicknefs with
which it removed the Kam's indifpofition,
only added to my fears. His fituation the
next day increafed my fufpicions : fcarcely
had he ftrength enough to appear in public ; but the art of the phyfician, by pronouncing it a falutary crifis, made the
fymptom pafs for the fore-runner of the
cure. Krim-Gueray, however, went out
of his harem no more ; and juftly alarmed
for his fituation, and the fafety of his Minifters, by making them partake of my
fears, I prevailed on them to make *Siropolo*
appear, to fignify to him, that his life depended on that of their mafter ; but this
chymift knew the character of his judges
well enough to be convinced, that their
ambition would foon be lefs occupied with
their

their dead mafter, than with the perfon
who was to be his fucceffor. No menaces
gave him the leaft concern; we were without hopes, and I had no expectation of
again feeing the Kam, when he fent to me
to come and fpeak to him. Introduced
into his harem, I found there feveral of his
women, whofe grief, and the general con-
fternation, had made them neglect to withdraw. I entered the apartment where
Krim-Gueray was lying : He had juft
finifhed different difpatches with the Divan Effendi‡. Shewing me the papers
which were lying round him, " See
there," faid he, " my laft work ; and my
laft moments I have referved for you ?"
But foon perceiving that my greateft efforts
could not conceal the poignancy of my for-
row, " Let us feparate;" added he ; " your
fenfibility would melt me, and I will try
to go to fleep more gaily !" He then made
a fign to fix muficians, at the bottom of
his chamber to begin their concert, and I
learnt, an hour after, that this unfortu-

‡ Secretary of the Council.

nate

nate Prince breathed his laft to the found of mufic. It is unneceffary for me to fay, what regret was occafioned by the lofs of him, nor how much I was myfelf afflicted. The affliction was general, and terror even took fuch poffeffion of men's minds, that they who flept the preceding evening, in the moft perfect fecurity, thought the enemy was already at their gates.

Whilft the Divan, immediately affembled, was difpatching different meffengers, delivering over the authority of the interregnum to a Sultan, and making preparations for the funeral of Krim-Gueray, *Siropolo* obtained, without difficulty, a paffport, and the neceffary order for poft-horfes, to return quietly to Wallachia. The fymptoms of poifon appeared very manifeft, however, on embalming the body; but the prefent intereft of that Court, ftifled every idea of vengeance, and of the punifhment of the offender. The Prince's body was carried into the Crimea, in a coach hung with mourning, drawn by fix horfes, caparifoned with black cloth; fifty

fifty horfemen, a number of Mirzas, and
a Sultan, who commanded the efcort, were
alfo in mourning ; and it is remarkable,
that the cuftom is no where in ufe throughout the Eaft, but amongft the Tartars.

The great fatigue I had fo long undergone, together with the uncertainty of my
fituation after this event, made me very
readily adopt the idea of going to Conftantinople, to wait fuch further orders as
might be given me : a part of my houfhold
was ftill at Baƈtchèferay, the other part I
had left at Kaouchan with Mr. Rufin,
charge d'affaires ; and I fet out with my
fecretary, a furgeon, a fervant, and the
Bachetchoader of the Kam, who had di-
reƈtions to conduƈt me, and was provided
with the neceffary orders. We were in the
Tartar drefs, and our baggage was in cha-
raƈter ; we had fcarcely enough to load
one horfe, which the poftillion led in hand,
and which we followed, riding poft ; but,
notwithftanding the quick trot of the Tartar poft-horfes, the diftance of the different relays prevented me from travelling
more

more than fifteen leagues the firft day. It
was ftill day-light when we arrived in the
village of Bafs-Arabia, which my conduct-
or made choice of for our abode ; he made
me ftop in the middle of a place, furrounded by houfes, and I remarked, that each in-
habitant, ftanding at his door, kept his
eyes fixed on us, whilft the Tchoadar,
ftaring about him, examined one after
another. " Well," faid I, to him, " where
are we to lodge ? Nobody feems to be
paying any attention to that."—" I beg
your pardon," replied he; " every body
is expecting, and wifhing to have the preference : by choofing the houfe you like
beft, you will be fure to make fomebody
happy." During this converfation, I obferved an old man, ftanding alone at his
door ; his venerable air interefted me ; I
decided in his favour, and had no fooner
made this choice, than all the inhabitants
returned into their houfes. The earneft-
nefs of my new landlord teftified his fatisfaction : fcarcely had he introduced me
into a low room, neatly fitted up, before
he

he produced his wife and his daughter,
both of them with their faces uncovered §.
The firſt carried a baſon and ewer, the ſecond a towel, which ſhe threw over my
hands, when I had waſhed them. Inſtruct-
ed by my guide, I ſubmitted, without difficulty,

§ We have ſeen that the law of Namekrem, of
which I have ſpoke in the Preliminary Diſcourſe, is
not ſcrupulouſly obſerved amongſt the Tartars. The
reader muſt have remarked alſo, amongſt that people, a great number of cuſtoms which ſeem to point
out the origin of thoſe cuſtoms which are analogous
to them amongſt ourſelves. Cannot we trace out the
origin of the nuptial crown, and the ſugar-plumbs,
which are common at the marriages of the European
nations, from the manner in which the Tartars be-
ſtow the marriage portion on the daughters ? They
cover them with millet : in the origin of all ſocieties,
grain muſt have been the received emblem of riches ;
in this light they placed a flat diſh, of about a foot in
diameter, on the head of the new married woman ;
they ſtretched a veil over her head, which deſcended
to her ſhoulders; after this they poured millet on the
trencher, which, ſpreading all around her, formed a
cone, whoſe baſe became proportioned to the ſize of
the bride : her dowry was not complete until the pyramid of millet reached up to the trencher, the veil
ſtill allowing her to breath. This cuſtom was not
favourable to little perſons ; they content themſelves,
therefore,

culty, to every thing which hospitality dictated to these good people. After ordering the supper, and leaving the women to get it ready, the old man, who until then had taken me for a Mirza, undeceived by the Tchoadar, came to make an apology for his inability to give me proper accommodations. My anfwer relieved him; and being defirous of afking him queftions refpecting the objects around me, I made him fit down, and fmoke, and take coffee with me, which was brought me by my fervant. This little civility, which he certainly would not have experienced from a Mirza, difpofed him to enter into converfation. I defired him to tell me why, for the fole purpofe of hofpitality, they fubjected themfelves to a cuftom, of which he

therefore, at prefent, with eftimating the number of meafures of millet that a girl is worth. But the Turks and the Armenians, who calculate in gold and filver, ftill preferving, however, the cuftom of the trencher and the veil, throw pieces of money on the bride, which they call "Spreading millet."—Why may not the nuptial crown, and the fugar-plumbs, have the fame origin?

he experienced, the inconvenience, and which was capable of ruining the richeſt individual, if the choice of travellers happened to fall frequently upon him.

The Old Man.

The preference you have given me, has only made me feel the pleaſure of obtaining it. We conſider hoſpitality in the light only of our advantage. The perſon amongſt us who ſhould conſtantly enjoy that preference, would make others jealous of him ; but we admit of no meaſures to fix the doubtful choice of the traveller. Our anxiety to appear at our doors, is only to ſhow that the houſes are inhabited.— This uniformity maintains the balance ; and my favourable ſtars alone have procured me the happineſs of your company.

Baron.

Pray tell me, do you treat the firſt comer with the ſame humanity ?

Old Man.

The only difference we make, is by going to meet the unfortunate, who are always timid, from diſtreſs. In this caſe, the
pleaſure

pleafure of affifting them is the privilege
of the perfon who can firft get hold of
them.

Baron.

It is impoffible more rigoroufly to fulfil
the Law of Mahomet : but the Turks are
not always fuch fcrupulous obfervers of
the Coran.

Old Man.

Nor do we think we are obeying that
holy book by exercifing hofpitality. We
are men, before we become Muffulmen;
humanity has dictated our cuftoms; they
are far more ancient than the Law.

Baron.

I obferve, however, that you have fome
modern cuftoms : for example, that bed
with four pofts, the tefter †, the bedding,
this

† The form of the Tartar beds I have juft been
mentioning, as well as that of the Grand Signior's
throne, which confifts likewife of a bed with four
pofts, prefents circumftances of analogy which may
appear interefting   When we confider that thefe governments muft have been Patriarchal, and that the
Tartars are in poffeffion of the moft ancient annals of
this

this table, thofe chairs, are they Tartar furniture ? or are they only to be found at your houfe ?

Old Man.

We know no other.

Baron.

I am the more aftonifhed, fince neither the Moldavians, nor the Turks, have any thing like them. I cannot conceive in what way thefe European cuftoms can have reached you. How happens it, that you have not adopted the Turkifh furniture, as well as your brethren of the Crimea ?

Old Man.

You fee accordingly fome cufhions, which our forefathers knew nothing of.—

this kind, as well as of many others, we fhall not be aftonifhed that the form of the bed from which their old men muft naturally have pronounced their judgments, fhould have been adopted, by way of model, for the Oriental thrones ; and if we add to this remark, the invafion of all Europe by people of Tartar origin, we fhall add the explanation of the term Bed of Juftice ; always employed in France, when the Sovereign Majefty difplays itfelf.

But

But corruption muſt neceſſarily make leſs progreſs amongſt us than in Crimea, where our Sultans ſhew the example of the Turk-iſh effeminacy, in which they are brought up in Romelia.

Baron.

I feel perfectly this diſtinction; but ſtill it throws no light on the origin of the pieces of European furniture I find here.

Old Man.

Nothing, however, can be more ſtrong-ly marked than the origin you are ſearch-ing after; theſe family moveables cannot be European; we are the elder branch; it is your furniture that is Tartarian.

This anſwer further excited my curio-ſity; I multiplied my queſtions, and had the pleaſure to hear my landlord confirm every conjecture I had myſelf already made on the ſubject. He informed me, like-wiſe, that the Tartars on the Caſpian ſea, and thoſe beyond it, preſerved the ſame cuſtoms.

The deſire of ſleeping on the borders of the Danube, obliged us to ſet out very early.

early. At my departure, my hoft proved himfelf true to the principles he had pro- feffed ; it was impoffible for me to pre- vail on him to receive the prefent I intend- ed to make him, for his kind reception.

We arrived at Ifmahel *, from whence I could not caft my eyes on the oppofite fide of the Danube, without thinking of the furly infolence of the Turks, amongft whom I was to be next day. The neigh- bourhood already partook of the infolence of their manners ; and this depofitory of the commerce between the Turks and the Tartars, no longer exhibited that good- fellowfhip, and that frank fimplicity, which charaƈterize the latter. Far from there finding obliging hofts, ready to affift you, one is delivered into the hands of induftri- ous, and greedy Jews, who are to be found in every fpot of the earth where there is a profpeƈt of gain, and they are fuffered to live.

* A town of Bafs-Arabia, on the left bank, near the mouth of the Danube.

Befides

Befides the favourable fituation of Ifmahel, as a depofitory for the tranfportion
of corn by the Danube, that town enjoys
a peculiar advantage, arifing from its induftry in the fabrication of the fkins of
fhagreens, which we call Turkey fhagreen.
Around this town are to be feen large
fpaces fet apart for the preparation of thefe
fkins. Firft, they are worked like parch-
ment; after which, they are fufpended in
the air by four fticks, which ftretch them
horizontally, and prepare them to receive
the impreffion of a fmall feed, of a very
aftringent quality, with which they are
covered; and after a certain time, the
fhagreens are found in a perfeft ftate of
preparation.

We had two branches of the river to
pafs before we could reach the other fide,
and it was fcarcely day-break, when the
ferry-boat landed us on the ifland, through
the middle of which we croffed diagonally
for four leagues, to arrive at the fecond
branch, over againft Tultcha, a Turkifh
fortrefs, fituated a little below the junction.

After

After providing ourfelves with horfes at
this place, we continued our journey
through a foreft, in which the poftilion
warned us to be upon our guard. But it
ftruck me, that five Tartars could never
be an object to excite the avidity of the
Governor's fon, and a few gentlemen of
his age, who, according to our guide's account, amufed themfelves with ftripping
the paffengers. We thought ourfelves out
of danger of thefe tricks, when, on coming out of the wood, we met a horfeman,
well dreffed, well mounted, and followed
by a ruffian, both of them covered with
arms, in a manner truly ridiculous. Two
carbines, three pair of piftols, two fabres,
and three or four great knives, made thefe
fellows imagine they had formidable appearance; added to this ftrange warlike
apparatus, they affumed a tone of infolence, defigned, doubtlefs, to frighten
timid people, and to enable them to judge
whether it would be prudent for them to
begin the attack. We faluted them civilly,
when they were within hail, and their

firft

firſt act of hoſtility was by not anſwering, concluding, from our tamenefs in receiving this fort of infult, that a few bravadoes would render us tractable, the rafcal who appeared to be the chief, takes a piſtol out of his armory, puſhes on his horfe, and kept wheeling round us ; but tired, at length, of feeing that the fellow wanted to frighten us, and reflecting likewife, that the opinion of our timidity might lead him to take fome ſteps which would oblige us to kill him, I thought it better to get rid of him by correcting his ideas. I quitted, in confequence, our little troop, and, piſtol in hand, I enter the lifts with this prancing gentleman. Struck with this manœuvre, he flackens his evolutions :—" Your horfe appears to me to be well broke," fays I to him, laughing, " but if he is of a good kind, he will ſtand fire ;—let us try :"— On which, I fired clofe to his ears ; the animal begins to rear, the cavalier throws away his arms, to hold by the mane, his cap falls off, and I left him in this fmaƚl confufion, which operated as a fufficient

correction

correction to them, and we quietly purfued our journey.

After paffing the plains of Dobrodgan †,
I obferved that the ground, which rifes
gradually towards the foot of the mountains which feparated us from Thrace, prefented, every where, great beds of marble,
which feemed to ferve as a bafis to the
Balkan ‡. We penetrated into thefe mountains by a defile, where the Kamtchikfouy,
(*the River of the Whip*) has its rife. This
torrent, conftantly fed by the fprings of
frefh water, falling in its courfe from one
rock to another, has fo many windings,
that it muft be croffed feventeen times before one arrives at the bottom of the defile,
where we began to afcend the mountains
by very difficult roads. We ftopped to
pafs the night in a village fituated about

† A province of Turkey in Europe, between the
Danube and the Thracian mountains, celebrated for
a fmall breed of horfes, much efteemed by the Turks,
from their being all pacers.

‡ The name given by the Turks to the mountains
of Thrace ; and, in general, to the higheft chains of
mountains.

the

the middle region, and had begun to take
fome repofe, when it was interrupted by
the noife of a numerous cavalcade. This
was the new Calga Sultan, brother to
Dewlet-Gueray, juft named by the Porte
to fucceed Krim-Gueray on the throne of
the Tartars. That Prince, who thought
I was ftill at Kaouchan, no fooner heard
that I was in the fame village, than he
fent for me, to wait upon him. He told
me that the Ottoman army was in march;
and after expreffing fome regret at the difference of our routes, concluded by prevailing on me to go a little out of my way,
to Seraî §, to fee his brother, the new
Kam. "He is preparing to fet out," added he, "and I hope, that by determining
you to return with us, he will make you
forget a lofs which you have thought irre-
parable." In fact, I did not believe that
the lofs of Krim-Gueray was eafily to be
repaired. But I refolved, without difficulty, to vifit the dependencies of the Tar-

§ A town in Romelia, dependent on the Tartar
Sultans.

M 2   tar

tar Sultans, that by feeing the manner of
living in Romelia, I might complete my
inquiry into every thing which concerns
that nation.

We had ftill to crofs the higheft chain
of the mountains of the Balkan. The fight
of their different ftrata, and the variety of
the rocks, which it feems to have coft
Nature an effort to rend afunder, to difcover the marks of the treafures they contain, prefent at every ftep, thofe great
characters, which enlarging our ideas of
the origin of Nature, call upon us to con-
template her works with additional intereft
and ardour. I faw in that part of the
mountains, the ruins of ancient caftles.—
I there obferved, too, numerous excava-
tions, fimilar to thofe I have remarked in
the Crimea, and which, no doubt, are in
the Balkan, likewife, fo many monuments
of tyranny.

Having reached the upper regions of
thefe mountains, we found there abundance of violets, whofe ftems and leaves,
hid under the fnow, formed a carpetting,

as

as ftriking, as it was agreeable. Continuing our route, we fell in with that newly
traced out by the Ottoman army. Its direction was towards Yffakché. This route,
marked out only by fome felled trees,
whofe trunks were left ftanding two feet
from the ground, to fave trouble to the
workmen, promifed fome difficulty for the
paffage of the artillery. Two little mounds
of earth, raifed to the right and left of the
road, repeated at ftated diftances, and always in fight of one another, were the
only marks in thefe plains to indicate the
route. I left this road at *Kirk*-Kiliffié,
(the Forty *Churches*). Whilft they were
providing horfes for me, there being none
left at the poft-houfe, the Turk who occupied the place of poft-mafter, endeavoured to confole me for the delay.——
He politely invited me to go up ftairs with
him, and after ordering a difh of *heavy*
coffee ‡, he gave me, in the interim, a
pipe ;

‡ An expreffion of the Turks, to fhow that they
do not fpare coffee. It is a very falfe prejudice to
imagine that the Turks are fond of weak coffee ; and

if

pipe ; and, to complete the regale, he gal-
lantly placed on the table a fmall piece of
wood of aloes.   This done, my hoft, bla-
ming the government for the inconveniencies I fuffered, began to talk politics ;
but tired with his prattling, I invited him
to fmoke with me, in hopes that this employment would flacken his difcourfe; on
this, he looks at his watch, reckons on
his fingers, and fays to me, " I will be
with you immediately."

A head, bending over his long neck,
the whole appearance of his perfon, which
was rather eccentric, had already made me
fufpeft that he was a lover of opium ; and,
in fact, he pulled out of his pocket a little
box, with a great air of myftery ; he then
claps his hands, to call one of his people,
fhows him his box, and this fignal immediately produced both our coffee, and his
mafter's pipe, which was preceded by a
large glafs of cold water.   The *amateur*

if they have given it weak to fome Europeans, it only
proves, that they were not inclined to treat them
well.

fmiled

fmiled at this fight, opens his box, takes
three pills, of the fize of three large olives,
rolls them, one after another, in his hand,
offers me as many, and on my refufal,
fwallows, with wonderful gravity, his
dofe of happinefs, which would certainly
have been fufficient to kill twenty perfons
amongft us. The time I was obliged to
wait for the horfes, gave me the opportunity of examining the play of mufcles,
and the fallies of imagination, which were
the prelude to that ftate of drunkennefs in
which I left this happy *Theriaki* †.

We had now reached Romelia, and had
no fooner entered the patrimony of the
Jengis-Kan Princes, than I was ftruck
with an appearance as rich, as it was different from the reft of the Ottoman empire. Variegated produ&ions in great
plenty, and well taken care of, country-
houfes, gardens beautifully fituated, a
number of villages, in each of which were
to be diftinguifhed the manfion of the Lord,
and his plantations, rifing up to the very

† Opium eater.

fummit

fummit of the hills, diverfified the face of
the earth, and formed a general landfcape,
in the European ftyle, the particular beauties of which redoubled my aftonifhment.

The town of Seraî now prefented itfelf
to our view, as well as the palace of the
Kam, where we arrived by a long avenue
in front of the buildings, and which conducted us to the efplanade that feparates
the town from the caftle. Several ftreets,
terminating like the radii of a circle, were
prolonged into the plain by plantations,
and formed a ftar, of which the firft court
of the palace occupied the centre. We
paffed this court, to arrive at the fecond,
where we alighted. I was firft introduced
into the Selictar's apartments, in one of
the wings. That officer, leaving me to a
few moments repofe, to take fome coffee,
which is the invariable cuftom, went to acquaint his mafter with my arrival, and prefently returned, to conduct me to his audience. We paffed through a large court-
yard, before we arrived at the wing occupied

pied by Dewlet-Gueray. Surrounded by
a great number of courtiers, he appeared
to be more taken up with the growth of
his beard, which he was obliged to let grow
from the moment of his elevation to the
throne, than with the arduous fituation
he was about to fill. I have had an opportunity of knowing, from a long converfation with this Prince, that ftill too young,
and perhaps of too feeble a chara&er to
tread in the footfteps of his uncle, Krim-
Gueray, he has no other ambition than to
devote himfelf entirely to the views of the
Grand Vifir.

It was too late for me, when I quitted
the new Kam, to think of proceeding on
my journey ; I accepted the offer which
was made me, therefore, to pafs the night
in the Palace, the more readily, becaufe
the Seli&ar who had charge of me, appeared to be of an amiable difpofition, and
fufficiently informed to refolve the queftions I wifhed to afk him on every thing
that had excited my attention. He informed

formed me, that this province, given as a patrimony to the family of Jengis-Kan, and divided into feparate territories, fecured to each member of that family hereditary poffeffions, independent of the Porte, and in which the right of afylum is inviolable. What was originally an acceffary to this grant, has eventually become the principal object. There is not a rafcal in the Ottoman empire, who does not here find impunity, provided he has wherewithal to pay the Sultan who protects him. To thefe windfalls, which are frequent, and the profits of which are collected in ready money, may be added, the tenths, the poll-tax, and the other domanial rights. The fortune of thefe Princes is further augmented by the produce of the employments fucceffively poffeffed by them in Crimea; but this emolument, limited by the Porte to the fole defcendants of Selim-Gueray, gives them a pre-eminence, from their opulence, over the Sultans of the other branches of that family, who, reduced

reduced to live on their patrimony, have vegetated, until this day, in the greateſt mediocrity*.

I left

* Selim-Gueray, who reigned at the end of the laſt, and at the beginning of the preſent century, after ſaving by his valour, the Turkiſh army, on the point of ſinking under the combined force of the Germans, the Poles and the Muſccvites, refuſed the Ottoman throne, on which the ſoldiery wiſhed to elevate him ; and the Grand Signior, to recompenſe the bravery and diſintereſtedneſs of the deliverer, ſettled the throne of the Tartars on his deſcendants, to the prejudices of the other Princes of the Jengis-Kan family. Selim Gueray obtained, alſo, the privilege of making the pilgrimage of Mecca, which no Prince of that Houſe had hitherto obtained. The Porte, in faƐt, might have reaſon to fear, that, at ſuch a diſtance, they would excite the people to revolt in their favour ; but Selim-Gueray's conduƐt could inſpire no diffidence. He made this pious journey, and his deſcendants have ſubſtituted the ſurname of Hadgi, (Pilgrim) for that of Tchoban, (Shepherd) common to all the family ; and which is ſtill preſerved by the other branches.

We ſhall be curious, alſo, to inveſtigate the origin of the ſurname of Gueray—always borne by the reigning Prince in Tartary. The tradition is, that one of the great vaſſals, whoſe name, and the æra of his crime, are neither of them preſerved, after forming the projeƐt of uſurping the throne of his maſters, and

I left Serai ; and the circuit I had been
forced to make to get there, having given
time for the Turkifh army to pafs Pazand-
gik, I met with nobody but ftragglers,
when I got once more on the direct road
to Conftantinople ; but the dead bodies
with which it was ftrewed, the plundered
ftate

and taking the neceffary meafures, gave orders for the
maffacre of all the Jengis-Kan Princes ; but that a
faithful fubject, availing himfelf of the tumult, had
the addrefs to withdraw, without the knowledge of
the affaflies, one of thofe Princes, then in his cradle,
and that he entrufted this treafure, and the fecret, to
a Shepherd of the name of Gueray, whofe probity was
univerfally acknowledged. The young Jengis, brought
up under the name of Gueray, faw, without knowing,
it, his inheritance a prey to tyranny, whilft his fuppofed father, occupied only with a country life, was
waiting the moment when the public hatred fhould
be fo matured, as to revolt the Tartars againft the
ufurper. The Prince had attained the age of twenty
when that event took place. The old Shepherd
always refpected, faw the confpiracy ripen, animated
the confpirators, prefented his Sovereign to the people ; and, after the death of the tyrant, re-eftablifhed
him on the throne of his anceftors.

Hitherto the new Kam had no other claim to govern them, in the eyes of the people, than the teftimony of a refpectable old man indeed, but who might
ftill

ſtate of the villages, and the general deſo-
lation of the whole country, loudly pro-
claimed the horrible diſorders which accompanied its progreſs. Bodies of cavalry,
and infantry were joining the army in each
other's footſteps, without officers, or the
ſmalleſt appearance of diſcipline. The little bands we met with, appeared only to
Vol. II.   N   be

ſtill be ſuſpected of acting from motives of ambition.
His diſintereſtedneſs ſoon diſſipated every injurious ſuſ-
picion. Called to the foot of the throne, to receive the reward of the moſt ſignal ſervice, he refuſes
all the honours which are offered him, and wiſhes for
no other favour, than to immortalize his zeal, by
rendering his name immortal. From that moment
he returned to keep his flocks : the Kam governed
under the name of Tchoban Gueray, (Shepherd Gueray) ; and the ſurname of Gueray is preſerved, to this
day, through all the ſucceſſion of Tartar Sovereigns,
as well as that of Shepherd, (Tchoban). The Turkiſh
hiſtorians differ on this point, and their compilations
would throw a doubt on the Tartar tradition, did not
the palpable falſehoods in the Ottoman hiſtories, reſpecting the moſt recent facts, oblige us to reject the
opinion of the Turkiſh annaliſts : They pretend that
the name of Gueray was borne by one of the younger
branches of Jengis-Kan ; but the origin of the proper name is not ſo much the queſtion, as that of the
epithet Shepherd. Now, we cannot trace the origin
of that name, but from the above tradition.

be got together to fquabble amongft themfelves; to fire away, right or wrong ; to
amufe themfelvès with the various acci-
dents arifing from their wantonnefs ; to
murder fome unhappy Chriftians ; to imagine their enemies already exterminated ;
and in their road, if I may be allowed the
expreffion, to gather the gleanings after the
crop ; but this was fo completely done already by the main body of the army, that
the remains of this horrible harveft were
to be traced up to the walls even of Conftantinople ; every thing was deftroyed
by fire; we changed our horfes on the
fmoaking afhes of the very poft-houfes ;
nor could we difcover a fingle habitable
fpot on this whole route, until we reached
the Seven Towers, where I alighted, to
go by fea to the fuburb of Pera.

Whilft they were looking out for a boat
for me, and were embarking our little baggage, a Turk, the news-monger of the
quarter, obferves me, and afks my conductor, who I am ? " It is a Mirza," replied he. The inquifitive fellow comes up

to

to me, and invites me to take fome refrefh-
ment : I accept the invitation, and we enter into a neighbouring coffee-houfe, of
which he was the orator. On a fign from
him, the place of honour is refigned to
me ; the company rife ; I ftride gravely
over twenty funnels of long pipes ; I feat
myfelf; and inceffantly regaled, and queftioned until my departure, I pay my fhare,
muttering a few monofyllables, from which
the politicians made very ingenious de-
ductions, and which gave great fatisfaction to the whole company ; nor was I
lefs fatisfied to leave them, to get to Pera,
where I loft no time in laying afide my
Tartar accoutrements.